Anxiety
Diary of an Ordinary Girl

Carrie Thompson

Anxiety Diary of an Ordinary Girl
Copyright © 2021 by Clarity Cove Publishing

Printed in the United States of America
First Printing, 2021

ISBN 978-1-948985-06-2
Ordering Information:
Quantity sales. Special discounts are available on quantity purchases by corporations, associations, and others. For details, contact the publisher at the address above.
Please contact Carrie Thompson at
carrie.elizabeth1987@gmail.com
Printed in the United States of America

DEDICATION

For all my soul sisters and brothers who have ever doubted their self-worth because of their mental illness and for all my Murderinos, Potterheads, Sloots, cat moms, unicorns, nerds and weirdos who spent their lives wondering where they fit in. Welcome to my tribe.

CONTENTS

ACKNOWLEDGMENTS

I don't know where to begin. There are so many amazing and lovely people who have supported me through this journey. First and foremost is my incredible family. Thank you for every single thing you've done for me my entire life, especially throughout my mental breakdown. I couldn't have survived without you. I love you so much.

To all of my incredible friends who have come to me throughout all stages of life, most of who have become family, I thank and love you too. To Sammi, Diana and Donna for being my first best friends and always sticking by my side no matter what. To Amber, my sweet friend, for believing in me more than anyone during this process, giving up your own time to help me and guiding me to the finish line. To Clarisse, Lynn, Mikey, my Dinos, Connie and Adasha for checking on me nearly every single day. I don't deserve any of you.

To Bria, Megan, Chelsea, Chelsea, Chelsea, Tina, Jen, and Kelsey for never letting me wallow in my sorrows too long. To my Linds for all your support and love. To my Gina, my forever roomie, for teaching me that I am so much more than my anxiety. To Kyle for answering me when I felt like I couldn't talk to anyone else. To my Leroy Fox family for bringing so much love and light into my life.

To Ashley for being the best therapist and friend that a girl could ever wish for, encouraging me every step of the way. And a most special thanks to my amazing book coach and publisher, Nicolya, my patient and incredible editor, Erica, my talented and sweet graphic designer, Christine and my marketing unicorn, Kayla. Without this team, none of this would have been possible. If I missed you, I promise I didn't mean it! You are in my heart and I'm forever grateful. It's just really hard to name every single person you know and love when you're lucky like I am to have a bazillion friends. Ha!

FOREWORD

"Progress isn't a straight line. It ebbs and flows. That's just how it goes." Thank you, thank you, thank you. As I read Carrie's words, I could not stop repeating, "This story is so important." At a certain point in everyone's life, I believe we hit a wall, a rut, a something that can only be classified as anxiety. Carrie's words put me back into the same era in which I underwent my own journey of reacting to having overactive anxiety in my life, and looking back and reflecting, Carrie's story helped me see the growth I underwent from the beginning of my anxiety to today, while reminding me the path is not linear. Some days, I am still anxious, however, these days, I am able to cope. Carrie's willingness to share her experiences, thoughts, feelings, reactions are all a raw hug that pulled me in and reminded me I was not, nor am I now alone.

During my own journey with discovering and dealing with anxiety, I remember bolting awake at 3 in the morning, feeling for my pulse, was my heart racing or did it stop beating? I remember countless EKGs thinking something was wrong with my heart, and I remember purchasing an Apple Watch because it meant I could do my own ECGs rather than continually going to urgent care. Carrie's book would have made the world of a difference if I had read it before or during, showing me my symptoms were "normal" and that there were other individuals going through the same cycle as me. There was nothing wrong with my heart after all, I needed to start with what was going on in my being and in my mind.

Funny enough, during this time, I sat across from Carrie in a corporate office, my desk facing hers. While I was battling out of body experiences in conference rooms on that very floor, I had no clue the poised, fun, put together individual sitting across from me was likely going through the very same things. Since then, and now that Carrie has shared her story, the two of us have been able to have open dialogue and conversations around the way anxiety has affected and can control our lives. Our journeys have been different, but one thing remains the same: we are in it together and that makes it that much easier to ride the wave.

Carrie's book exposed me to areas of coping with anxiety I was not familiar with and showed me the options that existed. Her ability to detail and provide new and different options for coping, coupled with her own personal anecdotes, create the perfect transparent space to expose us to ideas and situations we may not have explored ourselves before.

There is a statistic where 1 in 3 people have anxiety. These days, that statistic might be even higher. This world needs more people like Carrie, willing to come forward and lay her transparency on the table to get the conversation started. We are breaking the chains that shackle the topic of mental health into the category of "undiscussables" and Carrie's book is a start on the topic.

May you find solace in Carrie's words and know no matter what, you will get through. You are a diamond, and you are never alone.

With love and gratitude,

Amber Winton
Anxious Management Consultant + self-proclaimed mental health awareness promoter

PREFACE

Have you ever been in a room full of people, surrounded by friends or family and still felt utterly and completely alone? Stuck in your own head, thinking about how you don't belong or how no one could understand? Maybe you just feel broken and have no clue how to fix it. Well, I have, and that is why I want to share my story. My hope is to connect with others out there who feel the same and to also give them reassurance that they are not alone.

For much of my life, I felt like I didn't fit in or meet the standards of the people around me. I never felt this more than when I started my journey with Generalized Anxiety Disorder. Unfortunately, many people struggle with this chronically from a young age, but for me, it didn't really hit until I was in my late 20's. Sometimes life just creeps up on you like that and then hits you over the head with a giant sledgehammer. That's what it felt like for me. Mental health was never discussed in my family. I never knew anyone who had anxiety. I never knew anyone who was in therapy. I had never heard any good things about being prescribed anxiety medication and I didn't personally know anyone that was on medication. At least I didn't in the beginning.

When I first started mentioning my anxiety, people would tell me:

- "Just meditate."
- "Just breathe."
- "Stop worrying."
- "Do some yoga."
- "Take a walk."
- "Stay off your phone."
- "You're just stressed."

The list goes on and on. Because of this, I felt like something was wrong with me. I couldn't "just breathe" or "just do some yoga." Yes, those things are great when you get stressed and can help with anxiety, but it's so much more than that. No one ever explained to me that anxiety surpasses stress until I met my therapist. Stress has an identifiable cause and is something that you can possibly mediate. Anxiety has no source. It's just a little demon on your right shoulder that likes to get you up in a tizzy when there is no imminent danger or reason for fear.

Anxiety is biological for many of us. It's driven by the chemicals in the brain. Sometimes therapy and relaxation exercises will get you as good as new, but for many of us, it also means chemical assistance. My friends and family felt bad for me. I was staunchly against medication and thought "If I got myself into this mess, I can get myself out." Well, that's also not always true. With all that being said, I felt entirely alone, weird, and different. I was sad, angry, jealous, hopeless, worried, frustrated and half the time I felt like I was going crazy. Why me?! Why is this happening to me?! Everyone else is NORMAL.

I know that I'm not alone in having these experiences, although I felt that way for so long. On the surface, many people seem perfectly fine going about their everyday lives, but it's just not true. Social media paints so many unrealistic pictures for us. Hell, maybe the advice to "stay off your phone" isn't so stupid after all. The everyday appearances that people uphold don't always show the entire story. As a society, we are conditioned not to be weak or show emotion or talk about the bad stuff, especially when it's what goes on in your own head. It conditions you to feel like an outcast and it keeps you from having conversations with people going through their own battles.

Finally, I got brave enough to open my mouth and tell my story. I stopped allowing fear to own this piece of me. I want to leave the clichéd bullshit behind and talk openly about my experience living with anxiety as well as how I achieved personal growth while living with this mental health condition. I'm still working on it every day, but I'm here to share my story, give you some laughs, some insight, hope and courage to do the same. It's time to speak up and normalize mental health disorders. Hell, we are all a little weird anyway, aren't we?!

I also want to make it clear that I fully understand my experience may be different from yours. Perhaps my circumstances will seem much easier, more difficult or resonate entirely with your background. I acknowledge that I have been beyond blessed with the most incredible family and friends, a kick ass therapist, a job I enjoy, the sweetest kitty and many other privileges and blessings. I know that our stories may not perfectly align. However, I hope that through my story, you feel like you have a friend, someone to support you and someone who knows, for maybe even a short moment, what you're going through. Someone who just gets it. Mental health struggles vary across the board, but I truly feel there is something in those experiences that connects us all.

Now it's time to sit back and enjoy the ride. I want you to read this story, imagining that you and I are having a heart to heart over a cup of coffee...or wine because sometimes you need the strong stuff. I'm honored that you chose to join me, and I hope you enjoy the ride!

Carrie Thompson

Letter to Myself

I want to start this book with a letter I have written to myself. The following letter was a particularly painful assignment given to me by my therapist one week. It kind of serves as a synopsis of my book. This letter will open your eyes to the mindset in which I have been stuck for far too long. It will also give you a glimpse into why I felt compelled to write this book and share so much of myself. I know I'm not alone in how I've felt about myself, how I've treated myself and my circumstances, but I want this letter to serve as a reminder that how you view your circumstances and how you speak to yourself is immensely powerful.

I'm slowly learning that you have some control over your destiny and much of that begins with your mindset. Thought work is powerful, and I'm slowly learning, how to use it to my advantage. I've discovered there's not much in your life you can change without first learning to treat yourself with the love, respect, and kindness you show to others. As you read this letter, ask yourself if you've spoken to yourself like this lately:

Dear self,

There is so much I want to say, but how did you get here? You're a 33-year-old woman who just had to live with her parents, because she could not live by herself. Your mental health got so bad, that you couldn't even live on your own. You were like an adult child

1

and it took you months to even gain some sense of normalcy again. That is so embarrassing, and so frightening that you could even go back there.

Even though you have gained back some sense of normalcy, you're still far from normal. You are so anxious and fearful every day that it is ruining your life. You spend every day just waiting for the bottom to drop out, despite trying your hardest to believe that you're on the path forward. You constantly think something is physically wrong with you and you're terrified of getting some kind of chronic illness, because it's just one more thing to have to deal with and baggage for you to carry along. What if you never get back to a happy and relaxed life with a healthy level of anxiety and fear? No one would want to be with a crazy person like you. The only people you trust and are comfortable with are your parents, and they won't be around forever to hold you up. You are a burden on your family and friends. You used to bring so much joy, fun, and excitement and now you can barely exist to spend time with them. Where did that person go?

You're always trying so hard to impress other people. This had made you into an overachiever at work and in life. You're constantly trying to prove something or outshine people at work so that you will be recognized. You constantly feel guilty when you're not doing something 24/7 for fear of job security. Will you ever feel confident and secure in your job without the fear of being rejected?

You do this same thing in your friendships and relationships. You're constantly doing things for people and buying them things to make sure they care about you and like you. Maybe it's because you were always the fat, ugly friend struggling with your weight and your looks. Always looked at as second and third best, if that. Because of this you became anorexic in high school and got obsessed with working out. Still to this day you can't take a day off, even though your relationship with fitness and food has improved. Will you ever feel as if you look good enough or are enough?

Speaking of relationships, you should be married by now, but instead you're 33 and no one wants you. You've hardly ever been in a real relationship in your life. No one is ever attracted to you and if they are, you're always the side piece or get cheated on. You have used your sexuality to try to get attention, and that has never done anything positive for you either. With all of your issues, how will someone ever love you? You wake up anxious every day and sometimes have trouble convincing yourself to do things. You are too afraid to go on dates and aren't comfortable with anyone but close friends and family. You've turned into a shell of the person you used to be, and no one would want a lifetime commitment to that, which is proven by the fact that you're 33 and single with zero prospects whatsoever.

And let's talk about the medication. You swore you would never go down that path. How did things get so bad and so desperate that you reached this point? Who are you without the medication and who are you WITH it? Every day is complicated, and the process made a scar on you forever. Hopefully one day, this will all feel worth it for you.

You so deeply want to be the fun, sweet, adventurous, charismatic person that everyone wants to be around, but you're no longer capable. You are trying so hard to believe that this journey you're on with the medication and therapy will finally lead you to where you want to be, but it's very hard to fully believe this is true. Every day you're trying to figure out your purpose on this earth and how to fulfill it, but some days you can barely fulfill yourself. You used to believe you were meant to be a mother and wife and have a beautiful family. Now you just work and exercise to survive, wondering when you will find that "ah ha!" moment where you feel you've finally made it and made your mark. Instead, you spend your time being envious and jealous of the happy people around you with amazing relationships, jobs, and families. When will your moment where you feel truly whole and happy in life come along? Right now, it's so far out of reach, that you're just doing what you can not to lose hope.

Hopefully one day things will change and align for you, and I hope and pray for that every day.

Signed,

Me

So, what do you think? Have you spoken to yourself like this before? Has it been productive, or has it broken you down even further? After handing in this homework, my therapist read the letter aloud, and it brought me to tears. I was so sad for this person, this stranger to whom this was written. But that stranger wasn't a stranger at all. That stranger was me.

I hated myself. How had I reached this point? There was not one outstanding traumatic experience to blame. There were, however, lots of tiny wounds that began developing in my early stages of life. These wounds grew deeper and wider until they consumed my entire being.

I had become a shell of the person I wanted to be, and I wanted nothing more than to fix myself. Let's be honest, I wanted to wake up one day and realize it had all been one really bad dream, but that's not how life works. Now I fight day in and day out to try to regain a sense of normalcy and some confidence in myself in hopes of healing all my broken pieces. Some days are hard, and other days are harder. But, if I don't keep trying to push through, I know with certainty that I'll never see improvements.

I hope my story inspires you to give yourself some grace, love yourself a little more and never stop fighting for the life of your dreams.

THE BEGINNING

It's been kind of hard to figure out where to begin the story. Yeah, I know, it's my own story so how could it be difficult, right? We could say that I could start from childhood, I mean of course I can track some patterns back to that time, but that's not the true beginning. It all really begins when I started studying for the CPA exam. Before that time, I had the usual ups and downs that college students experience while living away from home and trying to start a career after graduation. Hell, I graduated from my undergrad at The Ohio State University (Go Bucks!) in December 2009, right in the middle of one of our most recent economic crises. That was a tough time for everyone, but back then anxiety was the last concern on my mind. The CPA exam, however, was a whole other beast that I couldn't have anticipated. It's also weird to be starting this writing journey today, because I'm sitting here in the exact spot where this began nearly five years ago.

Before we get to the crazy exam, let me explain how I got there. After graduating undergrad, I was living and working in Columbus, OH. I had a bar job and friends that I absolutely adored. I really wanted to start my marketing career, but I was too happy bartending and going out with friends to truly pursue my goal. I knew that if I wanted to break free of the service industry life, I'd need a big change. That change came in the form of moving to Charlotte, NC without knowing a single soul and trying to start a new phase in my life. The hunt for a marketing job in Charlotte wasn't easy. In fact, it was near impossible to find one. You had to have connections or know someone to really

5

get a foot in the door. Surprise, surprise, I went back to the service industry. For years and years, I cycled through various service industry jobs, a recruiting role and finally a supposed "marketing" job. That particular job ended up being more of a glorified administrative assistant role where women were treated like they were far less intelligent than the men running the business. After that, I got a short-term part-time bank teller role and got a part-time serving job until I decided to go back to school.

At this point, I was fed up with not being able to start the career I dreamed of, sick of being treated like I was stupid because I was a woman or a server/bartender and wanted a job with more long-term job security. I randomly decided that Accounting would be the perfect field. Many of my family members were accountants and my parents had analytical minds, so why not? Winthrop University was close to Charlotte and offered in-state tuition for graduate students living in the Charlotte area. My roommate at the time had gone there and recommended I apply. I took the GMAT, applied and waited for the acceptance. Once I was in, I met with a career counselor who was curious about my decision to make a complete 180 in terms of career choice. I told her I was confident in my decision, but she offered other options in case it didn't end up being for me. Luckily for me, I excelled right away.

While I was in class, it felt like the perfect fit. Being back in school gave me something to work towards and gave me a sense of purpose. I felt motivated and driven towards accomplishing my goal. I made a few friends that made it fun to come to class and my years there flew by. The CPA exam, of course, was a topic that came up frequently. I knew that if I was spending the time to get a Masters in Accounting, that I had to take the test. In my mind, there was no other option, even though many accountants find wonderful careers without it. My internship, and subsequent job offer with Ernst & Young the summer before graduation solidified the decision in my mind. Without a CPA license I could only advance so far, and now, there was also a bonus on the line if I passed. When you're working full time at your serving/bartending job and living on a tight budget, money talks. I was sick of asking for and receiving help from my family and couldn't wait to become more financially independent, although I have to note, I am so grateful to have had their help and support every step of the way. I never take that for granted.

Being the Type A personality that I am, I had the whole process planned out. I would graduate and then spend the next six months studying full time and taking the tests so that I was finished with the test before my full-time job with Ernst & Young started in July of 2016. I'd take one test in January of 2016, one in February of 2016 and two in May of 2016. Before graduation, I made sure I had all of the Becker testing materials and was ready to start. People always said, don't worry about getting more than a 75% on the test. That's passing. Employers don't care what your score is unless you get 100%, which for the record is near impossible. These words even echoed out of the mouth of the partner I'd be working for the following year. But, I'm a perfectionist. I studied for those damn tests like I was going to get 100%. If I could score 100% or more in my grad school classes, why couldn't I do that on this exam? I'm good at taking tests, so I thought I'd be fine. Little did I know what was in store. The study books are huge, the material is endless, and the practice exams could send you into a full meltdown, but I didn't realize this at first. In the beginning, it was really exciting. I decided to start with the Business Environment and Concepts section of the exam, which was supposedly one of the easier ones. This proved to be true, and I passed with no issue.

Next came the Audit section, which I allowed myself four weeks of study time after taking the prior exam. I had never excelled in the audit classes in school, so this just added to the stress. I have an analytical mind and prefer working with numbers. Numbers always give you an answer. There is no gray space. If you understand the concepts and how the calculations work, the answers come easily. Audit, however, was paragraph after paragraph of rules, concepts, processes, etc. It was basically like memorizing every word of a 400+ page book. Taking the test was even more stressful, and when I got back into the car with my mom to drive home, I immediately started to cry. This was where everything started sliding down hill.

After Audit, I decided to take the Financial portion of the exam because it was known to be the most difficult, contained the greatest amount of information and I had the largest window of time for studying and still get them done on the schedule I had laid out. I actually enjoyed studying for this exam, but the pressure to pass all three was starting to get to me. Right before going to take the exam for the Financial portion, I had my first ever panic attack.

Being the idiot I was, I got on Google and from what I read, I immediately thought I was having heart issues, which exacerbated the panic. I decided to jump in a freezing cold shower and drink a bunch of water before finally calming myself down enough to lay down and attempt falling back to sleep. I went to my GP's office and got an EKG. It turned out fine, and soon after she gave me a prescription for Xanax, explaining to me that she believed I had anxiety.

I was so confused, because I'd gone an entire 29ish years of my life without this ever happening. How did I get to this place? Well maybe the answer wasn't so obscure. Monday through Friday, all I did was study, sleep, and workout. Most days, I was studying eight or more hours during the hours of 9am to 9pm. I took breaks to eat and maybe go on a walk, or let's be honest, to get more coffee. On the weekends, I would work doubles at my bar job to make money. Some weeks, I worked myself to the point of tears. I lived off of coffee and 20mg+ of Adderall a day and was holed up in my dad's office for hours on end. I never saw my friends except when I was at work. There weren't enough hours in the day to make time for them, work and studying, which made me feel like a horrible friend, and I already felt like a burden on my parents and roommate for the daily support they were offering. But this was supposed to be the best way to do it, so I stayed the course.

I felt so lucky that I had the ability to do this, as many people have to work full time, as well as study. My mom (who is a saint) helped me with laundry and food. Because I came to their house Monday through Thursday most weeks to study, I was saved the time of having to cook or worrying about laundry. My roommate at the time, Kiersten, took pity on me and would help out with all the chores around our apartment. She would cook us dinner sometimes and always had a bottle (or 3) of wine on hand for the really tough days. She would send me funny videos or old pictures of us to bring a smile to my face. She listened to me bitch and always encouraged me, as did my parents. I honestly don't know how much worse it would've been had I not had that support system.

One of the mistakes along the way was telling myself that because I was given this opportunity, I had to pass. In my mind, there was no other option. All of my friends and family knew I was taking this exam. If I didn't pass, it was almost like I was failing them. Even failing and having to retake one exam carried an enormous weight that I was unwilling to contend with. I would have been so embarrassed, and at the time that felt like an unbearable outcome. This was all just an illusion, of course, something that I had tricked myself into believing for some time. My friends and family cared if I passed, but only because they knew how much it meant to me. At the end of the day, they would have supported me either way, but I couldn't convince myself to see or believe the truth. To this day, my mom believes I drove myself to insanity by putting so much pressure on myself and so much worth on passing these dang exams. At some point I loosened up a bit on this "life or death" thought pattern, but it would only come back later with a vengeance and consume most (if not all) areas of my life.

Anyway, I sloshed my way through the remainder of the study prep for the Financial section and went to take the exam. Through this time, the panic attacks increased in frequency. The worst part was that they'd come in the night like an unwelcome visitor. I'd be woken from sleep with my heart pounding out of my chest and my body flushed with heat. It continued to worry me to the point that I ended up in the ER for another EKG.

To take some of the pressure off for a few days before I really started studying for the final portion of the exam, I took a few weeks off of studying. Through the EDM scene in Charlotte, I had met some pretty rad humans. One in particular, Kory, was a special breed. This man went above and beyond to host the most outrageous and memorable gatherings. That spring he decided to rent out an entire camp in the mountains and throw a music festival for our friends. I was a little nervous to go away with a bunch of people I didn't know that well, especially with all my panic attack business going on, but I'm glad I did. Camp was one of the most incredible weeks of my life to date.

At Camp, we had the entire place to ourselves. Everyone slept in the houses or bunks on the campgrounds. It was just one big adult summer camp at its finest. We were up in the gorgeous Carolina mountains and the weather was perfect. It was warm enough during the day for a bathing suit and cold enough at night to be wrapped up in your favorite onesie pj's. The camp was up high enough that you could look at the surrounding peaks and valleys full of lush greenery. I got to spend time with friends from all over the US, met a ton of badass new friends, spent night and day listening to my favorite music, exploring the camp, participating in the activities Kory had coordinated and danced my ass off. Finally, I was surrounded by a bunch of weirdos just like myself and made some connections that would last a lifetime. Going home was depressing, but at least I was looking forward to one more trip before the studying returned.

A week after returning from camp, my parents and I went on a trip to The Wizarding World of Harry Potter. We only had about an 8-hour drive, so we made the trip on short notice about 2 weeks after I took the third exam. I am a huge Harry Potter nerd. You know, that kind that used to pre-order the books when they first came out and would wait in line at the bookstore to receive my treasure. I have watched every movie countless times and read the series every few years. Every day of that trip was magical, especially when I got chosen at Ollivander's Wand Shop to get a "custom" wand. Just when I thought the trip couldn't get much better, I woke up right at 2am on the day the test scores were released for my Financial exam and saw I had passed. I was elated but went back to bed and waited until morning to tell my parents.

The rest of the trip was amazing. We celebrated my passing of the exam and enjoyed our time away together. Mom even got me the Ravenclaw sweatshirt and Buckbeak stuffed animal I was eyeing as a celebratory gift. I know, I am a child. I thought that passing the third exam and taking a trip would eradicate the anxiety issue I had developed over the preceding few months. I was wrong. As I entered into studying for the fourth and final exam, the pressure only grew. The Regulation portion of the exam turned out to be the most challenging, even though I was going into tax. As my study days wore on, I became more and more burnt out. At some point, I finally stopped taking the Adderall in hopes that would help, since Adderall tends to make high strung people feel even more wired. This did not solve my problem. I was still waking up with terrible panic attacks throughout the night, so bad sometimes that I would drive to my parents' house at 2 or 3 o'clock in the morning. Eventually I headed back to my GP's office where she put me on Zoloft. Over the first week of taking the medication, we increased the dose more quickly than I now know my body could handle.

This led to extreme sadness, agitation, and suicidal ideations. I will never forget the day that it hit me the hardest. I had just gotten out of the shower and was planning to study for my exam when the feelings all hit me like a brick wall. It was one of the most traumatizing and frightening experiences that I'd ever encountered. I got dressed as fast as I could and drove to my parents. I remember thinking to myself "If you can just get to their house, you'll be ok." As soon as I arrived, I ran into the house and broke down, shaking, into sobs while my mom wrapped her arms around me. I remember telling her that I just felt so scared. And I was. I knew that I didn't want to commit suicide, but my brain was making me feel otherwise. It was almost an out of body experience.

For the following few weeks, I stayed at my parents' house at the request of my GP. I completely stopped studying and did little more than go on walks with my parents or run errands. This was also the point where I realized I probably needed a therapist. I'm not sure who recommended it, but I'm glad they did. My mom and dad helped me research reputable options in the area and we took our chances with the first one with an available appointment.

I seriously thank God for that day and maybe my mom's "motherly intuition" as she had selected her counseling practice. I had hit the jackpot. I was magically matched with who would become my "person" in therapist form. You know, that person you want to be friends and hang out with outside of weekly therapy sessions but can't really do that because of the rules. Therapy was really awkward at first, but Ashley (who I still see to this day) was a gem. She specializes in helping people with anxiety and would become one of my greatest resources off and on for the following years. Finally, I started to feel a bit better and got back in my normal routine.

After that few weeks of mental health drama, I cared less and less how focused I was and started to put in less study hours. I had pushed my exam back from May to July because of the break I had taken from studying due to my little mental breakdown. This means that some of the material I had studied in the beginning had been long forgotten or extremely hazy. But, by this point, the whole "I better pass all 4 on the first try or else" theory had been put to the test. Leading up to the day of my exam, my motivation decreased, and I stopped caring so much about the score. In my mind, all I could do was say a prayer and hope for the best. I had scored relatively well on the first 3 exams, reaching into the high 80's, but at this point I was just hoping to squeak by, and if not, oh well. Finally, I was ok with not passing and resigning to the fact that I'd have to retake a part while I was working full time. Let's be honest, I'm sure I would have had another full meltdown if this had actually materialized.

After taking the final exam, it was time to start my full-time job with Ernst & Young that July. I had one week to prepare to completely change my routine and relax before my first day. That almost felt like a relief, as I'd be seeing familiar faces and no longer spending my days studying alone in my room or dad's office. Waiting to receive my last test score was a long and painful process. Because of the time I had taken the exam, I'd have to wait over 4 weeks to know if I'd passed, as opposed to around 2 weeks with the others. Luckily, I had new hire training and onboarding to distract me.

Finally, after what felt like years of waiting, it was test score day. Woohoo! I should've known I would have good luck, because it happened to fall on one of my college best friends, Kathryn's, birthday. I logged in to get the score, and I HAD PASSED. Thank the Universe/Sweet Baby Jesus/Lord Above! You'd think I would have been jumping, screaming, and laughing for joy, but at this point I was numb. I was just grateful it was over, and I could move on with my life.

After all the exams were over and passed and my new job was in full swing that I'd be in autopilot with life. New job, no studying, time for friends, a steady paycheck, a predictable schedule, the whole shabang. I couldn't have been more wrong. Yes, I had a steady paycheck, but intro level public accounting pay isn't great. I kept my bar job on the weekend because I missed the lifestyle, secondly, I missed my friends, and third, I missed the money. Adjusting to my new routine and lack of interactions with all my besties was really challenging. I felt like I was having an identity crisis.

Do you know how hard it is to leave a job that you love with your entire soul, because you feel like you aren't being a responsible adult? Other than feeling belittled by older men in previous jobs (Hello, sexism!), this was one of the drivers behind my career change. I partially felt pressured by society to be in a corporate role, because bartending wasn't a "real job." There were no health benefits, job security, steady paychecks, predictable hours. It was fun work, and careers were meant to be serious. My brother and cousin had already found their niches in life and started their careers right after college. I was the oldest! How was I so behind? Behind my family! Behind my peers! How embarrassing!

I am smart, a hard worker and pick up quickly on any new skill, which pushed me towards a career in accounting, full of job security, a steady paycheck and 401K. But I'm also a free spirit, unicorn loving, nerdy goofball. I love to dance and listen to EDM music and (at the time) loved going to shows and festivals and partying with my friends. I missed having my own schedule, being able to go shopping in the middle of the afternoon with my friends (or the grocery store because that was prime time for shopping), working out whenever I felt like it, baking and cleaning at all hours of the day. Finding a way to blend the two parts of me into one and being proud of my whole being was terribly difficult and confusing.

Most of my peers seemed cut out for the office environment. They were more reserved and well-adjusted to the 9-5 life. I didn't think many of them would understand my free-spirited ways or my bold personality, which created a sense of isolation.

More than just the personality traits and life trajectory, I was older than most of my new staff and senior co-workers. I had chosen to go back to school for my Masters in Accounting in my late 20's, so when I started work I was 29. Most of my coworkers were fresh out of grad school and in their early 20's. Of course they like to go out, drink, watch sports, etc. Hello, they were in their early 20's, that's what a lot of fresh grads do during that phase of life (I know I did)? I was simply different though. Way more "out there." I wanted to dress up weird and go out with my other work friends. I liked going to EDM shows and had plans to go to festivals over the following year. I didn't want to go to the college bars. I wanted to go to the clubs to dance with my friends and see our friends DJ. All of this, and more, made me feel really alone and left out.

Some people told me that it was just time to change. That I needed to leave my "bar life" in the past and morph into this new human being who was serious and totally career focused. I think the assumption was that I would leave my friends behind and fully immerse myself in this new world, but like, no. This was something I struggled with for my first year and a half of my career.

Within a few months of starting my new job though, there was hardly any time to think about that. My first busy season was upon us. What we learned and experienced during our internship did not prepare me for the madness that would ensue. Because I chose accounting on a whim, I guess I didn't really do the research about what life as an accountant would look like. All I knew was that public accounting was the way to go when starting your career. The Big 4 firms looked best on your resume and would offer you the most learning opportunity and potential growth. Those facts are both true, and don't get me wrong, there were lots to love about my job in Big 4, but busy season was not one of them.

I didn't realize that busy season meant working Monday through Sunday, in the office preferably. It meant working from early in the morning until late at night, usually 12+ hours a day, and I was one of the lucky ones. There were people working 90-120 hours a week, which I could never do to myself. I had to have time to sleep and workout at the very least. Regardless, I highly disliked this new reality.

I did not want to work from the office on the weekends, but that's what my team preferred. This also obviously affected my ability to work at my bar job and see my friends. The question of my loyalty between jobs had come up on more than one occasion.

No one could believe I still worked a second job. I wasn't ashamed of it in any way and felt lucky that I had the opportunity. My beloved Leroy Fox had been my home all through grad school. The staff and owners supported my dreams and were along for the journey. Even if I didn't need the extra income, parting ways with that place would have been difficult. My regulars had become friends and with having a new office job, I missed the social interaction I got at Leroy's. I'm a social butterfly and love learning about new people, so I craved that contact. Still to this day, my Leroy's fam and my customers are like family to me. And hell, 8 years later, I even pick up a shift or two sometimes just for the social interaction and smiles.

I was doing fine balancing between the two, but God forbid I asked when our group wanted to come into the office on the weekend, because my priorities would be questioned. The constant scrutiny sent my stress levels spiking, because on top of already feeling out of place, now I felt like one more thing was "wrong" with me and that I couldn't be honest and myself. I hated having nearly every waking moment of my life being dictated to me, even my weekends. But that was life, and I needed to just get the f*ck over it. (Sorry mom!)

It wasn't all bad, ya know. Thankfully, I adored most of my coworkers. I sat and worked with a great group of ladies and had the type of senior manager that dreams are made of in public accounting. When you're stuck with people 24/7, you learn to love each other (for the most part, until you're sick and tired of seeing their faces every waking moment of the day). Over time we all became good friends, and I'd come to learn that I did have a kindred spirit or two around the office. We would take breaks for half price wine night during the week before returning to the office and try to take lunch breaks together when we had the extra 30 minutes. Despite being different and feeling out of place in the beginning, I learned a lot through this process and started to grow into more of a 9-5 (or in public accounting speak 8a-10p or so) professional. This is really what got me through the following year.

As I settled into my new reality, as unwelcome as it may have been, my panic attacks decreased, and I found my groove. That September, I had gotten the sweetest baby boy kitten, proudly named Albus Severus Dumbledore or Albie or Bubby for short, in September who became my whole world. He was a tiny little grey fluff ball, soft as silk and with a tail like a feather duster, with white on his face and little white boots on his feet. My favorite part was the little heart shaped black nose right in the middle of his white face. Having him around added so much joy to every area of my life. After a while, I stopped going to therapy and just assumed my life was returning to a state of equilibrium for good. Good riddance anxiety and panic attacks. Now that the CPA exam is over, you can get the hell out. Or at least I thought that's how life would progress, but I would later find out that my intuition about the anxiety matter was garbage.

After a year of working at Ernst & Young, the schedule was really starting to wear on me. I hated leaving Albie home by himself for 12 hours a day and had to have my dad go over to feed him every night. This also made me feel guilty, because my poor dad was driving 30+ minutes one way to my house every day to feed the poor guy or my roommates were taking care of him. On top of the long days at work, my commute was 45+ minutes each way, especially during rush hour. Most of the people I worked with weren't phased by these types of inconveniences, which made me feel like I just was not cut out for public accounting.

On top of the work drama, my roommates and I found out that we might be getting kicked out of our townhome due to a neighborhood restoration project. We were told that we would need to be out of our place by November of that year (2017.) This was an unwelcome surprise for many reasons, but mainly because I was so sad to be leaving the two most incredible roommates behind. Kitten would be losing his aunt and uncle, and I would be desperately missing my friends. Plus, I was potentially going to have to live alone. I was so used to having roommates and loved to come home and decompress with them after the long days in the office. No more would be our Sunday movie/wine/taco nights and endless amounts of laughs and stories. I entertained the idea of moving closer to the office, which would have been convenient in terms of commute and getting me closer to some friends and activities, but the rent in Uptown Charlotte for a one bedroom was astronomical. Instead, I decided to buy a place of my own, because if I'm dumping a whole paycheck on rent alone, I might as well invest and get me a mortgage payment.

My timeline (here I go again with the timelines) was to find a home to purchase and close on before the following busy season. This gave me about 4-6 weeks to find a home. I'm sure you have gathered this by now, but I am very impatient. I was up my realtor's ass constantly and stalked the MLS website she provided. I started seeing places right away and didn't love any of them. The one I did like would need a lot of work, and I had been outbid even when we did put in an offer. It was becoming increasingly difficult to leave work to go see home options, so finally my dad and realtor would just go check them out on their own. Eventually they found one that I was interested in. We put in an offer, and it had been accepted that night.

At first, I was so excited knowing that I had gotten my place, but then I had serious buyer's remorse. I had a full-on meltdown and my realtor had to call me to talk me off a ledge. I know these seem like silly first world problems that I'm lucky to have, but I believe that you can't put yourself on a scale with someone else. Judging your problems based on someone else's scale discounts what you are going through and leads to extremely negative self-talk. I'm telling you this story to show you how through my own set of circumstances, I developed the negative patterns that many of us suffer from. These singular silly or stupid moments add up to a much more serious issue and exacerbated problems I didn't even know existed. Sorry, as mentioned above I have ADD, so you might get a little sidebar every now and then.

Anyway, I finally calmed down and got all my ducks in a row before the closing date on my new home. I took the day off work to go to the closing and got my keys right before the 2017 fall busy season began. Unfortunately, a lot of work had to be done to the interior of my home before I could move in, so I would be trying to move in and unpack right at the beginning of when work was really picking up.

This ended up being a huge bummer, because once I got moved in, I hated being at work so much. I wanted to be in my new home unpacking, decorating and, of course, spending time with Albie.

This busy season would end up being my worst and my last. I was put on two separate assignments. One was a contract role with one of our larger clients, where I worked a strict 9-5 every day. After I had finished my work there for the day, I would log back on to my Ernst & Young laptop and work on my other client at night. While sitting at the client site for the contracting role, I realized what life could be like outside of public accounting. Damn, these people had it good. Some of them came in and only worked 9-4, taking an hour lunch in between. Industry had been the way to go.

One day, I opened up to my "boss" at the contracting site and expressed to her how I was feeling about work. She ended up linking me up with a recruiter she had worked with in the past, and I started to hunt for a new role. This was pretty easy to accomplish, since I wasn't sitting in my usual seat at the firm. I could talk to my recruiter whenever I liked and could go to interviews without being noticed. After a couple of interviews, some even at the client site, I had secured a new job and was beyond excited to start.

A part of me felt horrible, because I knew I was betraying my senior manager and my coworkers, but I had to do this for me. Thank God, they didn't hold it against me for too long, and we all still keep in touch to this day. On the bright side, one of my Ernst & Young coworkers/friends was already working at the company where I was headed. Knowing a familiar face would be there was exciting and slightly softened the blow of leaving my team. That October of 2017 I was ready to make this major transition, but I really had no idea how much of my old job I was about to miss.

STEPPING INTO NEW TERRITORY

For legal and personal purposes, no names will be used in this chapter or in the remainder of the book where it concerns material from this chapter.

You are probably wondering why I am giving you all this work background history, but it'll come to make sense soon enough. If you think about it, many of us spend the majority of our time in our place of employment or communicating with co-workers if you work from home. All of those hours will have an impact on your mental and physical health in one way or another, so it's important to find a welcoming and supportive environment. For a few years, despite loving the job, the environment wasn't all warm and fuzzy.

Now I want to ask you a question, even though I can't hear your answer. Have you ever worked in such a toxic work environment that you didn't know what kind of drama was going to materialize from day to day? Have you ever been mistreated off and on for years at a job, to the point where it was bad enough for you to wake up with feelings of dread about going into your place of employment? Well, that's what the rollercoaster of two or so years looked like for me. When talking about mental health, this is crucial and can be very damaging, and through this part of the story, you will see the toll it took.

When I first started the job it was exciting because I was much closer to home. My commute had shrunken to 15 minutes or so, I was making more money and the hours were exceedingly better. In the beginning I felt great about my decision to switch jobs because I was new, and everyone was trying to be welcoming and inclusive. I didn't notice all the drama right away, but it didn't take long for the smoke and mirrors to fade. Everyone in the group stayed friendly until they saw you connecting with someone they didn't like. As I learned more about everybody in the group, the truth about what was going on presented itself.

Thank God, the month before I started, the most incredible coworker started in our group too. She would become my rock, my sanity, and my work bestie over the next few months. She helped me laugh through all the craziness, and at least, we would try to find some humor in the madness that went on around us. Also, one of my favorite managers had started the same day as her and would end up being a lifeline for me.

The three of us were unique as we were fresh faces to everyone in our group and brought some new energy. I believe this was a bit of a lifesaver for our director because we came onboard untainted and drama free. Other than the three of us, the majority of the group had worked together in one capacity or another at some points in the years prior. Some of these individuals harbored an extreme distaste for one another based on past work experience. I often listened to my most hype music on the way to the office because every day was a mystery upon entering the building. It felt like gearing up for war on the elevator ride to our floor.

Now, I am sure you can relate on this one. No matter where you work, there will always be some interesting characters. There will be the older ones that think they are "above the law." I'll call them the "killjoys." The killjoys will come in late, take two-hour lunches, leave early and selfishly focus on their work and their work alone. And sometimes, they don't even want to do that. They always find ways to pick apart the other group members and are catalysts for drama. They tend to be conniving and undercutting when possible, and no matter how kindly they are treated, nothing makes them happy.

Sometimes I fall victim to these individuals because I love to be liked. I am a social butterfly and a huge people pleaser, so I am easy prey. I think the killjoys can sense my weakness and try to bring me to the dark side before anyone else can get my attention. They will be sweet and welcoming, but once they sink in their fangs, it is all over. Escape becomes dangerous and grueling.

We had a few of these. When my work bestie and I first started, they wanted to be friends with us. They wanted to make sure we heard their stories loud and clear before we made connections with anyone else in the group. These people would give us the hot gossip, or at least their tainted versions, and try to pull us into their drama. If they noticed us connecting with the other employees in the group, especially the ones they gossiped about, they got angry and offended, and were quick to treat us like we did not exist.

Then you have your average employee. I will call them the "bystanders." These types of employees mosey in around nine and creep out around five. My work bestie and I used to say they always seemed to have their "invisibility cloaks" on. What I mean by this is, whenever one of the managers or one of our leaders came looking for people to give work to, they conveniently disappeared. Heck, half the time if you were looking for them to ask a question or go grab a coffee, they were missing.

The bystanders would complete their assignments and dip out as soon as possible. They were not overachievers, nor were they extra helpful in times of need. Most of the time, these individuals stayed out of trouble and kept out of the drama, but their lack of enthusiasm and unwillingness to overly contribute sometimes made them the object of others' frustrations.

A few bystanders existed in our group. A benefit to having people like this around is that if you are trying to learn and grow in the group, opportunity always exists for you to pick up new assignments, because some people just do not want to take on more than the minimum. The bystanders allowed my best friend and I to take on more challenging projects more quickly than we may have otherwise been able to. Cheers to being overachievers!

Next are the dominant ones: The employees that clearly standout from the rest of the group by either skill, personality, work ethic, or occasionally, a combination of all three. Let's call them the "MVPs." The MVPs are natural born leaders. They get their hands involved wherever they can and are usually fountains of knowledge. They are well respected by leadership and are very dependable. These people let their personalities shine and try to relate to other employees on a personal level.

The MVPs are typically welcoming to new employees and enthusiastic to train and develop relationships. They have the best interest of the company and the group in mind. When seeking assistance, you always go to the MVP, because you know they will point you in the right direction. You want to get in good with the MVPs, because they can and will help you advance in your career and keep you motivated.

We had a few MVPs, and they were the people my bestie and I gravitated to first. They helped with our onboarding, development and relationship building with leadership. We could go to them with questions or for advice, and they would always lend a helping hand. They were personally invested in our growth and wanted us to succeed for the greater good of the team.

This is the group where I like to belong. I tend to have a big personality compared to my peers, for better or worse. I am also a n extreme overachiever and find I get along well with leadership. Networking with other colleagues and developing trusting relationships is one of my favorite parts of my job. And most of all, I love mentoring and welcoming new employees into my circle.

Last but not least, you have the quiet, hard-working intellectuals. I will call them the "dark horses." These people seem like your every day, run-of-the mill co-worker until you get to know them. They can be extremely intelligent, hardworking, charismatic, thoughtful, and natural born leaders. They keep their heads down, get their work done and always take on more than is required. They treat everyone equally and do their best to make the work environment fun. Dark horses are usually well regarded by most group members, leadership, and other business partners.

Working with a dark horse is a dream come true. They are sweet, helpful and absolutely brilliant. The way their minds work is incredible. They are innovators and problem solvers, always coming up with new and better ways to perform any and all work functions. The dark horses keep to themselves, but show enough of their personalities to be relatable, but only on a professional level. Becoming respected or mentored by a dark horse is the ultimate goal.

The dark horses in our group were my favorite people. Lucky for me, both of my managers belonged in this category and became lifelines during my time with the group. They supported my endeavors and pushed me to grow as a professional and as an individual. Any time I wanted to try something new, they made sure I got on the project and succeeded. During challenging times in my personal life, they stuck by my side and made sure I felt supported. For that, I am grateful.

Now that you have an idea of what my team was like, let's talk about the office. We worked in an open layout style office inside of an entirely glass building. Our section of the office had a lovely view of the top of the parking desk, although I would've preferred to be surrounded by foliage. The desks in our building were long, white and sat three people per side. They were double sided with a small two-foot divider in between you and the person across from you. Each of the three desk "sections" had an elevated square cubby and a set of drawers to either your left or right. These long desks sat back-to-back, so collaboration and chit chat were simple. You could just spin around in your chair and chat with the people behind you or say whatever you wanted to the person on the other side.

The offices were entirely glass, as well. Glass walls, glass doors, glass everything. Whatever anyone said or did, unless whispered very quietly, could be heard and seen by everyone, including our leaders. Even if you did whisper or talk quietly, anyone within close proximity could see your facial expression and hand gestures. Everyone could also see what was on your computer screens, as they weren't covered either, so it was best to keep your chat boxes to yourself and stay focused on work.

Now that I've set the scene, let's talk general group dynamic. My opinion was that the killjoys in our group tended to hate everyone. They would spread rumors about the MVPs and even sometimes the bystanders. Whether knowingly or unwittingly, they created drama amongst the staff and wreaked havoc for management. Some of these people brought over dysfunction from their prior jobs and allowed it to infiltrate our developing positive culture.

This type of environment was new to me. I had just left a very family-oriented and loving atmosphere and entered into a bit of a crazy situation. Culture was a huge deal to me, so when leaving my old job, I looked for a modern, inclusive, flexible culture, which the company provided. Our group just happened to still be working out the kinks.

Like I said before, in the beginning I drifted towards some of the killjoys. As I developed relationships with other employees, this started to become an issue, because if they saw you socializing with someone they did not like or respect, I felt like they would write you off immediately. And if they were really upset about it, any of the following actions might take place:

1. Talk shit about the other co-worker to you,
2. Talk shit about you to other people for being friendly with that co-worker or
3. Get mad and ignore you because you were being friendly with the co-worker. And if you were really special, sometimes all three could happen at once.

This situation may resonate with some of you because toxic work environments exist far too frequently. I think what made it so difficult for me was that I had come from a job where, despite the challenges, I adored my co-workers. We had all become friends, built meaningful and lasting relationships, and generally enjoyed each other's company. My bar job also had a healthy work environment. Rarely did someone join the team and not get along with the rest of the staff. When we fought, we fought like family, not enemies (which I'm sure in some people's experiences, those are synonymous). No one ever stayed mad for more than a day or two, and even when things were bad, you knew that in a desperate situation, they would have your back. My new environment left a bit to be desired at the time.

The behaviors and interactions I witnessed blew my mind. Killjoys would openly yell at managers on the work floor because they did not want to be told what to do. They would also get in loud disagreements with the MVPs and the dark horses for no reason other than they did not like the person. Name calling always existed. People were called conniving, jealous, self-serving…you name it. Leadership constantly had their work cut out for them, and despite the number of disciplinary actions taken, most killjoys would just continue on with their outlandish behavior. It was insane.

For a while, my best friend and I had a running joke that the office was like the Hunger Games. New players were constantly in the game and we always tried to guess who would make it out alive and why. As funny as that may have been sometimes, it was sad to witness grown people acting this way, but it taught me quite a few lessons. The bad blood constantly circulating made it difficult to get to see the truth about each individual and contributed to my anxiety.

On top of the occasional public displays of madness and aggression hinted at above, there was always the day-to-day gossip and rumor mill lingering in the air. It was a challenge not to get caught up in it, and I would be lying if I said I never participated. Alliances shifted every now and then and trying to keep on everyone's good side was rough. I did my best to remain neutral and be kind to everyone, although the neutrality waned as I got used to each member's work habits.

My general kindness never changed, but my tolerance level of certain people definitely diminished over time. In the beginning, some of the MVPs warned us about certain teammates. I should have heeded the warnings early on, but my people pleaser ways put me in quite the predicament. Wanting everyone to like you 100% of the time is not a great goal, especially when you personally do not love everyone either.

The teammates that created drama and caused disagreements

started to get on my nerves. They also tended to be the least motivated ones in the group, which would make me, and I am sure other coworkers, even more frustrated. I don't really do the whole astrology thing, but I'm an Aquarius, and I think I actually possess some of the traits. They tend to be independent, intellectual, free-spirited overthinkers. They also have a lower tolerance for people that lack motivation and drive, so that is probably why these individuals got under my skin so badly.

Over a two-year time span, these individuals would eliminate themselves from the group and allow for fresh, enthusiastic employees to come on board. As these transitions happened, a huge transformation began in our group. Each time a new person would join, it was like breathing a fresh breath of air. The stale, outdated workplace drama was replaced with enthusiastic, young minds. My new co-workers were career focused, kind and enthusiastic. Each one brought something new and positive to the group and were excited to be there.

Sadly, during these two years, I would go through an unfortunate set of circumstances with another coworker. To this day, I cannot pinpoint exactly what created the tension, mistrust, and awkwardness, but it was not fun. Our situation escalated up over time and on more than one occasion, made me want to leave my job. It probably did not help that I can be emotionally sensitive and crave validation from peers and superiors. But whatever...

In the beginning, I would gravitate towards this person. They were a fan favorite amongst leadership because of their knowledge and work ethic and were welcoming to myself and my work bestie. They dedicated a lot of personal time to get my bestie and I up to speed on details about the company and what we do in our group. Any time I had work related questions, I knew I could reach out to them for quick and accurate answers, as they were always willing to help.

My friend and I were both very hard working and ambitious, which made us favorites from the beginning. Because of this, the co-worker made sure that my friend and I were well positioned in front of leadership and set up to succeed. We all started to form a bond, and I was hopeful for the future of these relationships from a personal and professional standpoint.

At some point there would start to be cracks in my relationship with the coworker. Where they were still getting along great with my friend, something was off between them and me. My friend was quieter and kept to herself, where I had a more outgoing and bold personality, so maybe that was part of the issue. I tend to be overly friendly and love to dish out praise and compliments, which I guess could have made them uncomfortable.

At one point, I overheard the coworker complaining to other teammates about how I gave too many compliments and was too nice and they did not know how to respond to me. Maybe they just found me annoying, who knows. What I do know, is the rocky relationship continued for a long time. Sometimes we were getting along great. We would get lunch together, talk about shared interests or go run errands. Other times, I felt like my mere presence was creating a disturbance in their world. It was miserable.

As time went on, I felt like the chill/happy/peaceful periods of time became less frequent. As this happened, my anxiety got worse and worse. Many days I would wake up for work with feelings of dread because I just did not want to go into the office. Oftentimes I felt sick to my stomach and it would take everything in me to get through the day.

On a few occasions, it got to the point where I would have to speak to a manager. I felt awful for my manager at the time, because of the number of times she saw me cry. I would let the emotion bottle up for weeks or months at a time and then unleash it on her. (This is another Aquarius trait by the way. We hate to show emotion openly.) I always felt so embarrassed after we talked and hated that I had to involve them in any kind of drama.

On the worst occasion, something happened that caused my work bestie to be mad at me. I, of course, attributed it to something the coworker did, because I did not feel trusting of them at this point. My friend really would not speak to me outside of work-related topics for over a week. Now, not only was I feeling tension about the coworker, but my friend was not even there to be my wing woman. I was so sad and stressed over the situation that I finally broke.

That day, I asked my manager to go on a walk with me early in the workday. We ended up going out to the parking deck where we could talk in private. Thank God for that. I lost it. All the emotion and hurt burst out of me in waterfalls of tears. For the first few minutes, I could not even get coherent words out. After about an hour, we came back inside and continued with our day. My manager eventually talked to my friend and smoothed over the situation. After an apology and some time, everything was back on track and I felt better. But damn…that shit sucked and was so unnecessary.

Outside of the office, I felt like a burden on family and friends, because the situation at work was making me a party pooper. Instead of bringing fun and fascinating stories about my wonderful life, I was bitching about what was going on at the office. I felt like the only person there I could trust was my work bestie, and it just made me sad because I missed being surrounded by coworkers that were friends. It all really sucked and highly degraded my mental well-being.

At times, I referred to what I experienced for the first two years at this job bullying. It may not have been intentional and maybe bullying is not even the right word. Perhaps we just were not compatible, but regardless, I allowed this situation to become all-consuming for these two years and sent myself to a dark place, eventually leading to a complete mental breakdown. It consumed my thoughts every day, all day. I just couldn't shake it. There is something about being a people pleaser that makes me want everyone to love me, and I couldn't come to terms with the fact that life doesn't work that way. I'm sure there are very few people on this earth who are beloved by all, but (for some God forsaken reason) I'm convinced one of them should be me. We really shouldn't allow people who dislike or do not get along with us to dictate our behavior and how we feel about ourselves.

Regardless, it was very confusing and created a sense of panic every day when I woke up to go to the office. Despite the numerous conversations with my manager, and her going to talk to our director, the cycle continued over a two-year period. All would be well for a little while and then the world would seemingly come crashing down. Our group had a lot of drama at the time, so maybe some of their frustration (well, all of ours really) just ended up landing on me, but who knows. When we were in a good place, I felt so grateful. Other times, I just felt really hurt inside. It was like riding a roller coaster up and down constantly not knowing where you were going to be. This really started to wear on me, so I decided to go back to therapy in October 2018.

In addition to the chaos going on at work, life started heading into the slow and steady downward spiral that was 2019.

2019: ROAD TO A BREAKDOWN
(PART 1)

Around June of 2018, I decided to book tickets to a music festival called Holy Ship with three of my favorite humans, Emily, Taylor, and Louis. I had gone once before and had the time of my life. I am a huge fan of EDM, and this festival was one of the best in my opinion. You were on a cruise ship, so access to everything was at your fingertips. You didn't have to worry about sleeping in a tent or showering in public showers or going to food stalls to find food. The buffet was 24/7 and you could run back to your room any time you needed something, wanted to change clothes, or just needed a break from the dance floor. It was also a very intimate festival, because the DJs were all staying on board with you, so you would often run into them at each other's sets or just walking around the boat. I had a lot of friends going that lived in different states across the US, so this was just one added bonus. Now we just had to wait until January 2019 to get on board.

Between June 2018 and January 2019, I spent countless hours worrying about this trip. Traveling always made me a little stressed, but I think a lot of people feel that way. Festivals are a different matter for me. Music festivals are notorious for drug use. When I was younger, this didn't really bother me as I was naive and way more carefree. (Hey 25-year-old Carrie, where you at when I need you?) But now, it stressed me the heck out. Even though I was not participating in the drug usage, I was mortally terrified I would somehow get mixed up in a situation that would land me in jail. Not only that, but I was afraid that if I did end up arrested and in jail, that my beloved CPA

30

license that I lost my mind over would be stripped away from me.

Was this realistic? Probably not. Did it feel realistic to me? Abso-freaking-lutely. I am by nature a worst-case-scenario thinker. I think in therapy this may also be called *forecasting* and *catastrophizing* (See Ashley, I listen sometimes.) It is my absolute signature move, and I'm sure some of you can relate. This can be helpful at times, because when real life emergencies present themselves, we usually react more calmly than people who spend less time in the dark realms of their brain. But for everyday life, this shit is not useful.

Let's fast forward to January 2019. We had finally made it! The trip was less than a week away. After many conversations about my concerns, I was feeling excited about the upcoming festivities. I met Emily and Taylor out for pedicures and lunch so that we could discuss our plans for the trip. We intended on driving down the day before and needed to iron out the last-minute details. After lunch I was supposed to meet a friend for a first date and a few drinks before going home to pack.

When I got in the car to drive over to meet my friend, I started to feel a little anxious and my heart was starting to race. The drive from our lunch destination to the bar was about 5 to 10 minutes max. By the time I reached the parking lot, I was sweating, agitated and my heart was pounding. I checked my Apple Watch and it said my heart rate was 180 beats per minute! I freaked out.

I got out of my car and started to walk towards the bar. There were two people standing on the sidewalk, and I asked them for help. I told them I felt like I was having a heart attack. I was sweating, my chest was tight, my heart was going a million miles a minute, and I couldn't breathe. The lady had me sit down on the sidewalk and told me that I was pale as a ghost. The man called 911 while the lady took my phone and called my parents. Once she gave my phone back, I had to text my date to tell him I was sitting outside on the sidewalk. (Talk about embarrassing, but like, it doesn't stop there.)

Next thing I know a fire truck arrives. Now I'm in the center of a spectacle going on outside the bar. A friend of mine actually worked there and happened to be working the shift that night. She came out to see what was going on, realized it was me and brought me some ice water to make sure I was ok. The fireman did a little triage on me and said my heart rate was still 140 beats per minute, so we waited for the ambulance.

In the meantime, my date comes out and sits down next to me. Then my parents arrive, both in hysterics. I am holding it together by the grace of God. Then the ambulance comes. They bring me inside by myself and start to do their own work up. We start some deep breathing exercises to see if that will help anything, and it does not. My heart rate is not 120 beats per minute. It's coming down slowly, but not how they are expecting it to, so off to the ER we go.

As soon as they close the doors to the ambulance, I just lose it. I guess all the adrenaline kept the emotion in until that point. The two EMTs were incredible and so sweet. They start an IV of electrolyte fluids and hook me up to an EKG. The hospital is a quick ride away, so my parents and, strangely enough, my date follow.

Once in the hospital, a bunch more tests are run. They take quite a few tubes of blood, hook me up to another IV fluid drip, take chest x-rays and hook me up to a continuous EKG monitoring system. My parents and date are chatting away, and I'm just sitting there in stunned silence secretly freaking out because what the hell just happened?!

Eventually my date leaves (and then never speaks to me again after the incident...and my therapist wonders why I have such issues trusting men). All of the tests come back normal. The physician on duty comes to talk to me and tells me I'm good as new. He believes I had an episode of SVT (supraventricular tachycardia), which is a rapid heartbeat that develops when the normal electrical impulses of the heart are disrupted. It can come on suddenly for no reason and typically goes away on its own. This may only happen once in a person's life or may come back another time. I don't have a family history of SVT, so hopefully that one incident is the only I'll ever experience. He recommended that I schedule a follow up with my general practitioner and a cardiologist but says I'm perfectly healthy.

While he was there, I got all worked up about my trip. I was scared shitless by what happened and was concerned about leaving for the festival. The doctor tells me he definitely thinks I should still go as long as I get plenty of fluids and rest. I'm torn, but that's a decision for later. I'm finally released to go home, go to get my car, and drive back to my parents for the night. Still shaken up, I fall asleep and continue on like nothing happened. Except it did…

That whole little adventure to the ER had lasting effects. When I started having panic attacks a while back, I had developed an obsession with my heart rate. All too frequently, I would check my Apple Watch to see what it was, especially when I was uncomfortable. I kept an eye on it when I was working out, sitting down, working, sleeping, walking, etc. It was a terrible habit I couldn't break. The ambulance ride/ER visit compounded my obsession. This problem would linger on for over a year and on rough days, it still rears its ugly head.

Anyway, I decided to go to the festival and had the time of my life with my friends. Getting away was definitely good for me, and because I was going with my old coworkers, my heart was soaring the entire time. When we came back, I had my appointment with the cardiologist. They told me I would need to wear an event monitor 24 hours a day for two weeks. I was NOT happy about it. This thing was massive. The dimensions of the monitor were 6x3x1. Then there were the monitoring nodes stuck on my chest and under my boobs with wires hanging off all of them. The stickers irritated my skin and by the time the two weeks had passed, the rings around the nodes were bleeding.

Thank goodness it was January, because I could hide the monitor under big sweaters for the most part. However, at the time I was in a cycle instructor bootcamp and wearing it there was difficult. I discussed this with the cardiologist, and he recommended I disconnect the monitor and wires on bootcamp days so that my high heart rate didn't unnecessarily trigger the monitor. The node stickers could still be seen under my spandex, which made me insecure and embarrassed, but what else could I do?

Maybe by now you can see how I was starting to set myself up for a mental breakdown. I was working at my corporate job and my bar job and now added on cycle bootcamp with the intention of teaching as a third job. We were also in busy season at work, so the work hours were long, and then I spent the weekends at my bar job and bootcamp. I rarely allowed myself time to breathe or spend time with my loved ones. Fortunately for me, my friends know me way better than I know myself and could tell when I needed a break.

My birthday is in January and before my trip to the ER, I had planned to do a birthday get together at AR Workshop here in Charlotte. If you've never been, it's a DIY home decor workshop. Most of the pieces are wooden display pieces, like the kind you'd buy in any home decor shop. Picture cute inspirational paintings and seasonal signs to display around the home and outdoors. They also do canvas bags and pillows and hand knitted blankets and scarves. In order to decide when you want to attend a workshop, you go onto their website and look at the schedule. From there you can register for the type of DIY you're interested in trying.

For my birthday, I wanted to make a new wall hanging, so I chose a workshop that included wooden signs. My friends and I went online, picked out the size and pattern we wanted to work on and registered. I kept the group small, because it's kind of pricey and I would've had to reserve the entire workshop area to invite everyone.

By the time the weekend of my little "party" arrived, I wasn't keen on going anymore. At this point, I was on the heart monitor and feeling embarrassed about having to wear it. I was uncomfortable drinking alcohol (Hello, anxiety spikes!) and really struggling with my anxiety and some depression since the ER incident. I just wanted to spend the weekend with my parents and relax. I still spend most weekends with them.

My girls were not having it. Unbeknownst to me, my closest friends, some of whom had not even met the others, did some detective work, got each other's phone numbers, started a group chat and came up with some elaborate plans to get me out of the house for my special day.

First, Lynn and Kiersten, my old roomies, convinced me to go through with our plans to attend AR Workshop. We had already paid, so it made sense to go, and it would be nice to do something casual with two of my closest friends. Plus, when it came to Lynny, I always felt safe. There was, and still is, just something about her that gave me a sense of security that no one else could provide.

Lynn picked me up and we drove up to AR Workshop. When we were finished, she took me to Suffolk Punch, which is a trendy one stop shop that includes a brewery, coffee bar, amazing craft cocktails and seasonal cafe delights. The style is kind of steampunk meets farmhouse. There are long wooden tables and high metal stools. Viny plants hang from the ceiling and are nestled on shelves next to tiny decorative barrels. I always loved the aesthetic, and the seasonal dishes and cocktails never disappointed.

I told her I would be ok having a drink and some snacks and next thing I know, the best surprise happens. Four of my other favorite human beings showed up. Bria, Jen, Chelsea, and Megan were in cahoots with Lynny and Kier. What did I do to deserve these people? We all hung out having snacks and cocktails, and the birthday that I didn't even want to have ended up being astounding.

They also let me in on their little secret that night. Apparently, they had planned to basically break into my house while I was at work and surprise me if I wouldn't come out. Lynny had a house key and was prepared to involve my parents if necessary. After a few discussions, they thought better of it because they know me too well and thought it might create unnecessary anxiety showing up to a house full of people.

I was truly touched that they had put so much thought and effort into making me feel loved and important. Because I was in such a rough patch of life, I had stopped seeing and talking to people and holed myself off. This would become a worsening pattern over the remainder of the year, but they always stuck by my side. This wouldn't be the only time they pulled me out of the dark space in my head and the second time would mean even more.

Let's go back to this whole cycle instructor obsession. Being a cycle instructor was a dream of mine, especially at the studio where I auditioned. Eight of us made it through to the bootcamp, but there weren't teaching spots available for all of us. This made every bootcamp session like a competition. There was so much pressure. My natural perfectionist tendencies and competitive nature magnified the pressure for me, especially because in order to participate in the bootcamp, I was forced to quit the cycle instructor job I had secured just a few months earlier in September 2018.

One of the major issues for me was that I thought the coach played favorites. If there was a potential instructor that wasn't as strong as the others, but she liked how they looked on the bike better, she favored and put more time into mentoring them. I think favoritism is a part of human nature, but in circumstances such as these, I think it's best to attempt an unbiased approach. From the beginning, I got the vibe that she wasn't excited that I was in the training class and thought that would definitely hinder me. All that could have been made up in my head (which wouldn't necessarily be shocking), but I was pretty convinced. Being a people pleaser and always craving validation from others, I wanted her to like me and take interest in my development. I felt there was little I could have done to increase her interest in my success.

I tried to form friendships with everyone else in the training class and offer support whenever possible. There were times when other people wanted to quit, but I would try to encourage them to stick it out. Sometimes people needed music suggestions or choreography ideas, and I would offer up suggestions. I would keep personal conversations to myself because that's really no one else's business. And a lot of them did the same for me. That's how team relationships should be, right?

Now, I'm not some saint. Obviously, we all have judgmental bones in our body, and I'm not exempt. I didn't connect with some people on a personal level and some I didn't think were cut out for the job, but that wasn't for me to decide. Occasionally I voiced these thoughts to the people I trusted but tried to keep it to a minimum. I genuinely wanted everyone to succeed. We all felt like a little family at this point and watched each other's growth. However, as the training progressed (by the way, this training was like 3 months long), the competitive feelings started to creep in and occasionally felt like an "every man for himself" type scenario. Maybe that's because I didn't feel supported by our trainer, and I can only speak for my personal experience.

Overall, I think the trainee class did a great job of celebrating each other's wins and lifting each other up through the losses. I formed some incredible friendships that I'm beyond grateful for and acquired some fun memories. I also learned important lessons about accepting and utilizing criticism and responding instead of reacting. I'm definitely not the best when it comes to being judged critically by others, but this opportunity contributed to my personal growth.

Unfortunately, near the end of bootcamp that spring, I got cut before final test out rides. My unenthusiastic approach to accepting criticism was one of the issues. Another time while I was in the studio, in a moment of immense frustration, I said that I was never stepping foot in there again. I had felt discriminated against at this point, so I just cracked. I'm not proud of my behavior whatsoever, but I let my emotions and my hurt dictate my rash behavior.

I was also betrayed by someone who I trusted. One of the girls that I had immediately connected with turned out to be extremely self-serving and either didn't consider the consequences of her actions or didn't care. She was definitely the most skilled in our class but found the need to gain respect and popularity by throwing me under the bus. She took private conversations we had, twisted my words, and used them against me to our trainer and master trainer. I could not understand why! I also left a group chat all the girls were in because it was blowing my phone up when I was on a weekend trip to Chicago to see my BFF Gina. She shared that as well and made it out to be this big deal when I really just wanted my phone to stop going off. It was all bullshit in my opinion. Those actions ruined any chance of a future friendship and really hurt my feelings. Like what was the point in doing that?

To this day, I'm still hurt by her actions and will never understand why she did what she did. Of all the girls in bootcamp, I thought we'd actually become good friends. Now, I should probably mention I don't have empirical evidence that it was her, but the process of elimination was quite simple. I have also, on numerous occasions, tried to discuss what happened with her, noting that I wasn't mad but just wanted clarity, and she just ignored me. This to me screams "I'm guilty and don't want to own up to it," but ya know, I could be wrong. The mystery of what happened still bothers me a bit to this day and that betrayal will always lie beneath the surface.

In addition, I felt betrayed by people at a studio I had loved and supported from the day their doors opened. I also felt I had let myself down in a major way. I let the training, the competition and pressure get the best of me and affect my level of professionalism through the process. There are some decisions I regret, but I think at the end of the day I dodged a bullet. The day I got cut was almost a relief, at least for a little while.

After a bit, the jealousy and self-deprecating internal discussions began. What could I have done differently? Why did I trust those people? Why did I quit my other instructor job for this crap? Why do I have to be so anxious and put so much pressure on everything? Why can't I just live with what happened, move on, and still enjoy my love of cycling? All this swirled around in my head for the remainder of the year and still gets to me sometimes. But I have learned from the experience that it's ok to fail, and sometimes failing really works out for the best. During this period, I was nursing torn labrum injuries in both my hips (and still am), so this probably actually saved me some long-term physical agony.

Once the whole cycle bootcamp incident passed, I went back to focusing on my two jobs for the remainder of the spring and summer. It was nice to have some of my time back and to be able to pick up shifts without worrying about time conflicts. I had a few months where I eased off worrying about the heart issues and focused on stockpiling some extra money for a trip to Europe I was taking in August. I had already paid for the majority of the trip, since I'd saved for YEARS to go, but extra cash never hurt. I was still going to therapy and still anxious, but not every day was rough, so I let my guard down and kind of got lackadaisical with my self-improvement efforts.

A nice break came in May for Lynny (and her fiancé Bry's, who was also our roommate and someone I adored) co-ed bachelor/bachelorette party in New Orleans. This was a personal test for me to see how I'd do away from home, in large crowds, staying out late drinking and partying. My anxiety tried to creep in, but I told myself that the weekend wasn't about me, it was for Lynn. She had been my rock for years at that point, and I wasn't going to miss the opportunity to celebrate her and Bry. She had also introduced me to all of her best friends from Illinois while we lived together, and I couldn't wait to spend time with them either.

Kiersten and I arrived Friday evening, but everyone else had arrived earlier that day. We rushed to the hotel and changed for dinner, because I couldn't WAIT to see the bride-to-be and my friends. I ended up staying out late that night, which was a major deal for me because I hadn't done that in ages and woke up without anxiety the next day (WOOHOO!)

Despite some unnecessary drama that arose that weekend, which didn't involve me, it was nothing but super fun times. I drank at my own pace (A.K.A got drinks and gave most of them to other people) and left to go back to the hotel whenever I wanted. Heck, I was proud that I'd made it through most of the day Saturday trekking carefree around Bourbon Street. And to top it all off, that Saturday I found out that one of my favorite Illinois couples, Kelli, and Jeremy, were expecting a baby! What more could a girl ask for?

After the weekend was over, I stayed in New Orleans for an extra night and got to spend some quality time with my favorite little spiritual goddess, Taylor Rose. She was expecting at the time and just five months earlier she and her husband adopted the most perfect little boy, so we snuggled on the couch and binge watched tv. By the time I flew home the next day, I felt recharged and my heart was overflowing with love. Lynn, knowing that this was all a huge step for me, even texted me to tell me she was proud that I stepped outside of my comfort zone.

While my personal life seemed to be improving, life at work was getting worse. Since I began having the issues earlier the prior year, both of the managers I had during that time had done what they could to remediate the personnel issues I was having or at least did what they could to help me focus on my future with the company instead. But, I'd finally reached the end of my rope. Walking into work every day had become like a game of Russian roulette. I never knew what to expect. Maybe my coworker would be friendly today or maybe my existence would get on their nerves. I hated it. I didn't understand it. I knew they were a good and caring person, so why were all of these uncomfortable moments occurring? Some of it was probably my paranoia and oversensitivity, but still I freaked out every day going into work and quickly resumed my search for a new job.

At this point, I had told my boss I was intending to leave the company. I could no longer stand how I was being treated. As a last-ditch effort, my managers advised me to seek guidance from a less biased source. It felt like the right thing to do since nothing else had helped, so that summer I reached out and they scheduled a meeting with me. Talking to someone I was not close to and did not already trust was extremely uncomfortable for me, and it made me feel like I was doing something wrong. I never imagined I would have to take these measures but was hopeful it would bring change.

At the meeting, I expressed my concerns about how my coworker would react to bringing in outside help and feared it would impact my job even further. The contact told me that he could see in my face how afraid I was and promised that my job was safe and that I had made the right decision. Despite what had happened, I didn't want to hurt their feelings or cause any problems for them and their job, which heightened my fears. I continued with the meeting, which lasted about an hour. When we were finished, they offered me reassurance that everything would be ok and promised to be in touch after they spoke with my managers and coworker.

I wasn't sure what to expect, because my coworker was well respected in our group. Both of our opinions mattered, so both of our voices had to be heard. I did not want this to end up being a "their word versus mine" situation, although that was kind of the only possible outcome. I am very conflict averse, so having to go through this process was not ideal. I also possess a low level of patience, so waiting to see what the outcome would be was taxing on my mental health.

Because I sought help outside of our immediate group, I was hoping my identity would be kept anonymous when they went to talk to my coworker. But due to our relationship and basic common sense, it did not take much for my coworker to figure out that I had put them in this awkward position. Office life went from bad to worse. I could feel the tension in the air every day and felt extremely anxious when we had to collaborate. I can understand why they would have felt upset and hurt by my choice to speak to someone, but at the time, I felt backed into a corner and made my decisions based on that feeling. This would go on for a while, but at least I had full backing of support from my managers, family and friends. After a few months, everything settled down and the air began to clear. I'm glad I stuck it out through this time, because the improved relationships and improved work environment was what I had been craving all along

Until the work environment improved, the other work-related difficulty was the guilt I felt for being such a sour puss every day. Let's be honest, I literally hated going into work every day during this period despite enjoying my work and the company of my team. My main motivation was the paycheck, but I'm infamously an overachiever, so I couldn't let myself (or my team) down by slacking off because of how one human was making me feel. I tried to channel all my energy into work, but that was not always easy. I often left work feeling exhausted and defeated, already worrying about he next day.

My work bestie was always there as my rock and listened to all my rants and whining. Honestly, both of us were a little miserable at the time because we were supposed to be getting promoted soon but saw no signs of it actually happening. We had busted our butts and worked hard to outperformed employees above our level. We both received positive feedback time and time again, but we were ready for our promotions and raises. I tried to remain hopeful that my boss and director would make this happen for us, but was starting to lose some faith (and, of course, patience). Waiting and waiting just heightened the feelings of frustration I was already experiencing.

Really, though, I felt like my pissy attitude was letting down our new staff member who was to work closely with me. He was fresh out of school and would be working closely with my boss and myself. We wanted to give him the best experience so that we could train and retain him. I have to say, I was impressed from the beginning. He was still young and definitely got distracted easily but was extremely intelligent and took on challenging tasks without batting an eye. He had to get used to our working hours and the amount of work that would come during busy season, but it was an absolute joy to work with him.

He had an easy-going personality and was willing to learn anything we threw at him, which made him extremely valuable. I also think our few male coworkers let out a sigh of relief knowing that they were no longer surrounded by only a flock of women all day and had the new guy to discuss sports and video games. Plus, we were all happy to have an extra body to do the work.

In addition to his contributions as a coworker, he turned out to be an incredible friend and work bestie. Sadly, in his first few months, he'd hear some of my bitching, because of my overwhelming daily anxiety, but I felt confident that his experience would be nothing but positive, full of learning and networking opportunities. He was also new and pliable, so that would make him a coveted resource. I would try to talk up the job and make him feel as welcome as possible, which was partially made easy because we had the best manager in the entire universe, and I tried to make sure that the good always outshined the day-to-day frustrations.

I mean, hell, he started in May, during the height of my unhappiness and frustration. Obviously, I was in a dark, rough patch and my mood wasn't always the most upbeat. That shit actually bothered me, because I am notorious for being bright and sunshiny most of the time but take note: this is a facade put on by many with mental health issues. Dark on the inside, bright on the outside. Get to know people below the surface level. You never know the impact you could make. Thankfully, he stuck it out, grew his knowledge and made us proud. He also brightened the workplace up quite a bit for me and helped me to stick through the next few troublesome months.

Like any season of life, I'm happy to say this one eventually worked itself out, and I'm so grateful for the leadership and coworkers that hung by my side the entire time. I'm glad I pushed through the painful times because I loved my job responsibilities and my team even more.

As I reflect back on this time, I realize I learned a lot about overcoming adversity and staying strong. When life was hard or things didn't go according to plan, I used to give up so easily. Now, I try to push through, reminding myself that bad times don't last forever. Being patient and reciting positive affirmations over and over can make a world of difference.

I have also learned that you cannot trust everything you hear. Sometimes people will tell you things that sound good just to make you feel better. Those things might not always be factual. And most importantly, I've learned that open and direct communication is the best way to solve any issue. I encourage going directly to the source. There you will find the most honest and valuable information and may create change you did not know was possible.

While I was chugging along and waiting for my work environment to improve, my personal life offered some relief from the work trauma, and the next few months would be full of adventures. A special weekend visit with my best friend Jennifer in Houston, a lake day with my festival friends here in Charlotte and 4th of July weekend visit from my brother. Then one of the more exciting and unpredictable parts of my year was to come in late July.

2019: ROAD TO A BREAKDOWN
(PART 2)

Late that July, one of my favorite humans on this planet, Katie, was getting married to her soulmate, Evan. I felt honored to be on the guest list as they were only having their closest friends. The wedding required me to travel to Seattle, but I was thrilled. Traveling to and exploring new cities and cultures is one of my favorite past times, so I was looking forward to my first visit to the Pacific Northwest. It also didn't hurt that some other friends from around the country would be flying in for the festivities as well, so it was bound to be a weekend full of love and happiness.

I flew in the night before the wedding and got to spend some quality time with my friends, meet some new faces and dance the night away. Our friend, Maya, and I decided to share an Air B&B. The day of the wedding, we woke up ready to explore the neighborhood we were staying in and did so before getting ready for the wedding. Once we got all glammed up, we grabbed an Uber to the venue. When we showed up, I was in awe. They'd chosen to get married at Golden Gardens Park. (Google pictures if you've never been there.) The actual building location of the wedding was right on the beach with the water just a few yards away and the mountains in the distance. With the back doors propped open, we could see the scenery from inside and had easy access to the beach beyond. The weather was Seattle summer perfect, warm with the sun shining and barely a cloud in the sky. They could not have picked a more beautiful day.

We had arrived considerably early, so I got to spend some extra time with the bride and our beautiful friends who were helping her get ready. When we first entered the venue, I noticed a tall, handsome gentleman behind the bar but didn't think much of it right then being that I was just visiting for the weekend. After a few moments, I was pointed back to where Katie was getting ready and spent the rest of my time with her and our friends Lisa, who was doing her makeup and Kendall, her best friend.

An hour later, it was go-time. Katie looked absolutely stunning, and watching Evan get his first glimpse as she walked down the aisle, my heart melted. The emotions didn't stop there. They read each other, what I consider to be, the most well thought out, heartfelt vows I could ever imagine. There was truly not a dry eye in the place. I had never been so moved during a wedding ceremony, and I'm sure many other guests felt the same. By the time they were officially pronounced wife and husband, the love vibes were flowing through the building. To this day, I tell Katie that I have never felt an energy like what was circulating during her wedding and reception. It was otherworldly.

The reception was a ridiculous kind of fun. Most of these people were friends from attending music festivals over the years, which means eclectic, magical, weird, fun, adventurous humans. Once the ceremony was over, most people changed into bright, colorful outfits and the drinking/dancing began. (Let's be honest, most of us had started drinking prior to the ceremony taking place.)

After a few too many cocktails, I got some type of courage I had never possessed before and told the bartender, Brad, I thought he was cute. This led to some kissing and spending the rest of the evening hanging out by his side, even though he was working the bar. Apparently, he had asked Katie about me earlier in the evening, so this couldn't have worked out better. He got my number at the end of the reception and came to the afterparty with us. Then we spent the rest of the night talking and getting to know each other. (Don't worry. He wasn't some kind of stranger, weirdo. Katie had worked with him before and knew he was a good dude.)

The next day when I went to leave, I felt kind of sad to be leaving. Dating in Charlotte was (and still is) an onerous process. Why did I finally meet a man I connected with that just happens to live 3,000 miles away? This sucked, but I had already planned to come back to Seattle soon to visit Katie and Evan. There was so much I had yet to see, and I wanted more alone time with them, so why not fit him into the plan. I was going to be in Europe for the last two weeks of August, so I planned to return in early September.

Over the next month we would talk every single day. We texted, we called, we FaceTimed. Unlike regular relationships where you can see the person whenever it was convenient, we had to rely on technology and our communication skills. Because of these long daily conversations, we learned so much about one another in such a short amount of time. The connection we were building was much deeper and more genuine than the surface level connections I had made with people here in the Charlotte dating scene, so I fell too fast. I felt weird about it, since he didn't live here and we had only spent a short amount of time together in person, but I couldn't help it.

I've always had this fairytale idea about relationships and love. The majority of my life I had been single, and friends always told me that because I waited so long, when the right one came along, I would just know. (More on the whole dating nonsense to come.) I wasn't so sure I believed them all the time, but a part of me always hoped they were right. Living with these ideals in the back of my mind was a very slippery slope.

Because I was starting to develop some feelings for Brad, I didn't let my trip to Europe disrupt our daily chats. He was basically along for the ride with Aaron and me. The trip filled the deepest desires of my soul. For years, I wanted to go on a European vacation and after lots of saving and planning, I finally got to go. No anxiety, stress, OCD, Type A hang ups were going to stop this trip from being memorable.

I couldn't have picked a better travel partner. In late 2018, I asked my friend Aaron if he wanted to join me. He is a grade A human/friend that shares my passion for travel. When he said yes, I was elated. I knew he was reliable and wouldn't back out at the last minute. In early 2019, after all my heart drama had initially passed, we started to book our trip and decided on seeing Prague, Munich, and Rome.

Finally, August 14th had arrived, and it was time to head to the airport for our journey across the Atlantic. Brad was not happy to learn I was going on my trip with a man, but after several conversations about how we were just friends, he dropped the subject. Aaron and I arrived in Prague on August 15th, jetlagged but ready to explore all that Prague had to offer. In order to try to beat the jetlag, we had scheduled a beer tour for the first night. The group only had nine people, including the tour guide (Hey, Lenka, you rock!) and one of the couples was from Charlotte. Obviously, we hung out with them all night and met up again during our time in Prague. What a small world.

During our visit we wandered the streets of Prague on the search for history, craft cocktails and food. We stopped in Olde Town Square to see the Astronomical Clock, wandered to the John Lennon wall (basic b*tch photo op, duh!) and, of course, checked out one of the crazy museums (Sorry, Aaron. The sex museum wasn't the best idea.) In addition to the famous landmarks, the craft cocktail scene piqued our interest. Black Angel's Bar and Anonymous Bar were our favorites, but nowhere seemed to disappoint. Prague was charming and certainly lived up to its hype.

After a few days, we would head to Munich, which turned into quite the adventure. About an hour into the train ride, all the passengers were asked to leave the train, as there were issues with the track ahead. We were all dropped off in the middle of the Czech Republic where no one spoke a lick of English (including most of the passengers). I'm sure you can imagine, but I was near tears having a full-blown panic attack. How in God's name were we going to get to Munich?! Cab? No! Uber? That shit doesn't exist out there!

We were, however, informed that we were to catch a bus to another train station to then board another train to Munich. All the signs were in Czech or German, so we couldn't decipher what we were supposed to do. At some point, the crowd started leaving the platform where we were dropped off and rushed to the station below. Of course, we followed.

Once downstairs, everyone was just kind of huddled in the bus area. Yay! Buses! Maybe we could figure this out. I was still freaking out but had this strange pull to a girl about our age sitting near us. I asked her if she spoke English, and by some grace of God she did. Then I asked if she could help us and she said yes. Her name was Ellie. Ellie spoke to a group of guys nearby who seemed to know what was going on and reported back to our little group.

We finally boarded a bus and then hopped on another train to Munich. I was so grateful for this girl and even happier to spend the next few hours with her. Once we got to Munich, I couldn't just let her go without some kind of payment. After we dropped off our luggage at the hotel, we met her at the Augustiner-Keller, the oldest biergarten in Munich, for dinner and some beers. We all had a lovely time at dinner, took some pictures, exchanged contact information, and promised to keep in touch. I'm so happy that to this day, we are still friends, and I can't wait to visit with her again.

After that anxiety inducing incident, the remainder of the trip was perfect. We toured around Munich for a few days, and I fell in love with Germany. I have a deep love of history and have read a lot on WWII, so visiting the Dachau Concentration Camp Memorial was one of the first stops. It was almost like a dark cloud hung over us for the duration of the tour. The atrocities committed within those four walls were unthinkable and, at points, brought tears to my eyes. The German people, however, show such reverence for the victims and show deep remorse for acts committed in the past. Thank goodness we decided on a beer tour to close out that evening, because we needed a pick-me-up. Coincidentally, we had the same tour guide for both activities, so we all got a little chuckle out of that.

We visited Neuschwanstein Castle, rumored to be the real-life inspiration for Cinderella's castle. What a stunning sight! While we walked through the rooms, I felt like I was living in a fairytale. After the castle stop, we traveled through tiny German villages that were reminiscent of every Christmas card I'd ever seen. Red roofed homes that I would just picture to be covered in snow. The surrounding mountains, which were located at the edge of the Swiss Alps, vast lakes and spruce forests were majestic. The whole experience was enchanting. On the bus ride back to Munich, I wanted to close my eyes from exhaustion, but I just couldn't let myself miss a moment.

My favorite moment of the entire trip would come when we did the bike tour of Munich. I gotta be honest, I almost backed out last minute, because I was afraid to ride a real bicycle. I indoor cycle all the time, but this is totally not the same thing. Thankfully, the tour guide was patient and encouraged me to give it a go. I'm quite sure Aaron wanted to kill me by this point.

I was a natural. Biking through Munich was such a freeing experience. We rode through gorgeous gardens, past historical sites and even stopped to watch some urban surfing. I felt like a kid again. We had one last dinner before we headed to Rome and chose the Ratskeller. The only reason this is really important is because, that night is when I tried to end things with Brad. I was starting to question the legitimacy of our "relationship." Was he really as he seemed? It was all roses and butterflies over the phone, but was this sustainable in reality? That night he fought for us. He told me he wasn't going to let me throw what we had away. He was in it to win it and was sure we could make it work. It all sounded great. He said what I needed to hear, but later on I'd come back to this moment and question my decision.

The next day we headed to Rome and the Amalfi Coast for the final days of our trip before heading home. We saw all the touristy sights you'd imagine. The Colosseum, the Vatican, the Trevi Fountain, and the Spanish Steps. The highlights for me, of course, were the two trips to my favorite place in the world to get ice cream (gelato), Giolitti, and dinner at the incredible Imàgo. What a way to go out with a bang. Saying goodbye to our hotel before sunrise on the last day was a major bummer. By the time we were boarding our last flight back, I was exhausted but already missing Europe, especially Germany. Now I had to prepare to head back to the office and for my journey back to Seattle.

Now you can start to see why I kept my bar job. 2019 was bound to make me broke. I was so blessed to be able to afford these trips, but part of the payment was neglecting my personal wellbeing and mental health. My parents, friends and therapist all scolded and warned me that it was too much, but I never listened. My only focus was the money so that I could afford all the bachelorette parties, weddings, and personal trips I'd planned. But in a few months, I was going to learn a serious lesson.

Ten days after I got home, I jumped back on a plane and headed off to Seattle. I could not wait to see Katie and Brad but was feeling a little anxious about finally seeing him again. The first night and entire next day, my anxiety was soaring. I didn't sleep well, and my mood was definitely affected. A nice long hike definitely helped to perk up my mood. The trails were stunning. Being surrounded by lush greenery and hundreds of years old trees paired with the cool 60-degree weather was just what I needed. Midway through our hike, we stopped at a beach to rest and eat snacks. After, what seemed like, a never-ending summer in Charlotte with weeks spent in the office or behind the bar, a cool breeze on the face and the beauties of nature did something to my soul.

That night Katie, Brad and I adventured out again. Evan was working, so our first stop was his restaurant. Then they showed me to some of their favorite bar spots in the neighborhood. What started out being an awful day, turned out incredible. Katie and I might have even busted out singing Backstreet Boys at some point. (Quite frankly, this was one of the best parts of the day.)

The next day, I woke up feeling spectacular. Being the sweetheart he was, Brad took me to Orangetheory so I could get in a workout before starting the day touring Seattle. After the workout, I got ready and we headed to Pike Street for brunch and for him to show me around Pike Place Market. Wow! I had heard good things, but this place was a spectacle. To this day, I owe myself another trip out there because there was just too much to see in one day. Afterwards he took me to his brewery, and we stopped at a few places for cocktails. At some point during the day, we decided to make our relationship official. I felt some type of satisfaction knowing that my intuition to stick this out was right. At least I felt that way at the time.

Going home the next day was really hard. I didn't want to leave Seattle, but missed home, especially my baby kitty boy. I desperately wished I could take Katie and Brad (and ok, you too Evan) home with me, but that's just not how things were. This is where the logistical issues would begin. How the heck were we going to make this relationship work? I mean, he lived 3,000 miles away. Yeah, the phone was great and all, but not being able to touch, hug and see your person is really effing hard.

A few weeks later he would come visit and meet my friends and family. He was the first person I'd ever introduced to my parents, so this was kind of a big deal. They loved him and so did my friends. I had high hopes for the future of our relationship. He treated me like an absolute queen and dealt with my anxiety fairly well, at least he did in the beginning. In my entire life, no man had ever treated me with that level of care and respect. I was used to being cheated on, lied to, used, treated as a convenience instead of a priority and left with a lot of heartbreak. Trusting men and letting my guard down didn't exist.

Maybe that's why I fell so fast and so easily. He seemed perfect....at least for a while. Like I said, while I was in Europe, I tried to cut things off. I thought to myself "What are you doing, Carrie? This can never work." But he fought for us. He fought so hard. Hard enough that I was deluded into thinking that we could make this work. He sent me the sweetest messages and always made time for me. Until he didn't.

I wanted him to come to Lynn and Bry's wedding with me a few weeks after his visit, but of course he couldn't. It was his busy season at work. He was the Operations Manager of a trendy and popular microbrewery in Seattle. Dry hopped season at the brewery was the peak of their business. At least that's my understanding. New brews would be released, and the Seattle brew scene would be on fire. He couldn't get out of work for, at least a few more weeks, so there was no chance. At this point, we were both trying to figure out when we would even see each other again.

Tensions were growing high, at least from my point of view. The day that he turned off read receipts on me (yes, I know this is psycho to think about but WTF! I'm your girlfriend supposedly), I knew it was a sinking ship. He got sassy with me about how he couldn't text me back while he was working and communicated less. My stress, anxiety, and overthinking about how we could possibly make this work long-term was getting the best of me. He told me that I was like two separate people sometimes. Sometimes I was loving and sometimes I was distant.

He started to be distant too. He pulled away. Then one day, he asked me why I was so stressed and if it was about the distance and time apart, and I said yes. Right then he proceeded to break up with me over text message, telling me he could never see himself moving to Charlotte and that he knew I'd never leave my parents in the Carolinas. I was beyond upset. He then tried to call and make it all ok. I was not ok. I actually felt a little blindsided. We also had a trip to meet in Denver for a little getaway together in a week's time. We decided to still go on the trip as friends, but I should've backed out right away.

I thought the trip would give me closure. It did not. I cried the entire time. Yeah, Denver was great, and we had a lot of fun, but I was miserable inside. Why, oh why did I put myself in this position? While we were there, he told me that at least I now knew how I should be treated by a man. I felt like he was just patting himself on the back. Yes, he did treat me exceedingly well, but he also hurt me pretty badly. Sometimes I wonder if he just said it to make himself feel better.

Anyway, we went our separate ways and decided it was best not to really communicate for a while. Occasionally, one of us would reach out to say we missed the other, but generally, I just spent time in my own head dissecting what the hell I had done to myself. A small part of me held out hope that by some miracle we would get back together over the holidays and figure out the logistics, but that was my heart speaking not my brain.

The remainder of October and beginning of November were uneventful. I was sad, but because Brad wasn't in Charlotte, I could focus my attention elsewhere. Albie and I caught up on a lot of snuggles, because I kept leaving him for trips. The only thing I disliked about travel was missing that little pipsqueak. The highlight of my day, every day was/is snuggling up with my little cuddle buddy. That was all going well until my work bestie finally found a new job and put in her notice.

Here's the thing. My best girl at work and I were told that we would be looking at promotions back in September, and when the time rolled around to receive the promotions, they decided to promote someone in our other office whose stint with the group was shorter than ours. And even better, no one even warned us. So, we found out just like most other people in the group, when the email went out congratulating him.

She and I both really lost our shit. We were already both unhappy with how things were going in our group, me especially, because of the workplace bullying nonsense I had been enduring, and were considering looking for new jobs. I had lightly searched, gone on one interview and had a meltdown when I found out I didn't get it. My girl, however, was more persistent. She deserved much more than she was getting. More appreciation, more money, more flexibility. She had more experience than I did to begin with and was an incredible employee. After interviewing at a few prospective new employers, she accepted a new position.

Part of me was jealous, but at this point, I had detailed conversations with my boss and our director about my future with the company and had decided to stay, barring improvements of the culture of our group and a promotion in February. I enjoyed my direct responsibilities and loved my boss, so I was willing to give them one more chance. The other part, the bigger part, of me was devastated. My work bestie was my saving grace and sanity every day of work. Coming into the office would never be the same without her, but I was beyond happy she had found a place that would treat her how she deserved. At least I had our new guy as my new partner in crime once my best buddy was gone.

With my girl having left me and work slowing down, at the last minute, I decided to go to Chicago the first weekend in December to visit my girl Gina and her boyfriend for their annual Christmas party. I figured this might be the pick-me-up that I needed to boost my spirits. I always had the best time with them. Chicago is one of my favorite U.S. cities, and Gina has been one of my best friends since our college roommate days. The trip wasn't going to include anything extravagant, just us getting back to the good ol' days of grocery shopping and hosting parties together. I couldn't wait to spend time with her, because seeing her is always good for my soul.

The night I got there we went to eat at Happy Camper, one of my favorites and then off to the grocery store. We didn't get home until 2am from the store, so I went to bed shortly after. The next day was party time. We started out with a good workout and then came home to prep. By the time it was party kick off, I was feeling a little bit anxious, but wouldn't let that ruin the fun. The night was a blast, but around 1am the anxiety crept back.

You see, I have this issue surrounding bedtime. If I do not go to bed by a certain hour, I start feeling a little out of sorts. I ended up curling up on Gina's bed with her good friend Amber, who is such a calming force. We ended up having a heart to heart and it left me feeling much better. I passed out that night and woke up so sad to have to leave the next day. Visits with Gina are just never long enough. This was the last time I'd really have some fun before the real trouble began.

Life is full of surprises, you know, and I was about to get one of the most unwelcome surprises of my life.

THE COMPLETE UNRAVELING

December is supposed to be joyful, merry, and bright, right?! I love Christmas time and after going to Gina's party, I was fully in the spirit. Who am I kidding, I'd been in the spirit since November 1st. Reality is, the mountain of stress, anxiety, and emotion that I'd built up over the last 12 months was all about to start crumbling.

Back in July, my therapist had me do a neurotransmitter test, because my anxiety had gotten so bad and we were trying to figure out why. Based on this test, my brain chemical levels were all out of whack, specifically my dopamine and serotonin. My levels were way below average levels. Now, I know the accuracy and legitimacy of these tests are controversial, but I was desperate.

After receiving the test results, at the recommendation of my therapist, I decided to begin the vitamin regimen they recommended to help bring my levels up to normal. I was hopeful that this would solve my anxiety issues, because, from my understanding, the vitamins would also act like an anti-anxiety medication. The company constructed daily pill packets that contained breakfast, lunch, dinner, and bedtime vitamins that I was to take daily for as long as it took to restore my levels to normal. I started the regimen in August and would continue for a few months until life got a bit out of control.

The week before Christmas was a terribly busy week for me. I had Cookbook Club with my girlfriends, my work Christmas party, volunteering at Levine's Children's hospital and was working both jobs. If the week would've gone as planned, by the following Monday, I would've worked for 14 days straight and stuck to my personal obligations. This may not seem that bad, but it was a lot for me.

Over the last few years, I'd become a homebody. After work, I wanted to come home and relax, so having these holiday time obligations was already making me feel overwhelmed. Stack on top of that all the weekends I'd been working and my already diminishing amount of free time and you have the recipe for me to meltdown. The first reality check came while I was at my volunteering activity.

I was so excited to be back volunteering at Levine's again. In 2018, I'd signed up through work and got to help separate all the toy donations provided to the hospital and assist in writing Thank You notes to the donors. It was such a great experience that I had to do it again.

The morning started out fine. I arrived, checked in and said hello to some familiar faces from the prior year. However, when the program facilitator started to explain the manner in which we were to separate and box the toys, my heart rate spiked out of nowhere. I started to feel extremely hot, shaky and couldn't breathe. Because this had happened before, I pulled one of the nurses that were helping us aside and asked her to come sit down with me. I explained that this had happened before and that I was ok, but I needed to sit down for a few minutes. Another nurse brought me a huge glass of ice water while I sat, and after about five minutes, I told her I could go back in to start my work.

I still felt pretty shaky, but I didn't want it to turn into some big scene in front of the other volunteers from my office. Of course, I checked my Apple Watch like the psycho I am, and my heart rate at the peak of the episode was around 150 bpm. I stayed pretty freaked out the rest of the morning but tried to get through the day.

Then the volunteer facilitator decided to take us on a tour of the hospital. I love Christmas, so I was pumped to see the decorations and some of the facilities available to the children and families that spend so much time at Levine. The hospital is such a magical place. They have this dangling, multicolored glass display hanging in the lobby that is so beautiful and eye catching. Because it was the holidays, they also had a giant, elaborately decorated Christmas tree near the welcome desk. On every floor there is a "Santa's Workshop" type room that is filled with toys for children of all ages to choose from. The parents are also able to come to this room and "shop" for their child. The hospital also houses a resource library for parents to come and research their child's illness with the assistance of a librarian, so they aren't on their own to find accurate data from home. During the holidays, this room is decorated like a child's holiday fantasy, kind of like a candy land. The hospital definitely lives up to its reputation of being an outstanding facility for the treatment and care of sick children and their families.

The tour started fine, but as soon as we got in the elevator, I felt the weird full body freak-out starting to come on again. By the time we reached the top floor, I was very overheated and felt like I might pass out. This certainly took away from the experience, but I tried to hold it together. I mean, at least I'm in a hospital, right?

At this point in my life, I was still not fully convinced that I didn't have some type of heart anomaly that was causing these "heart racing issues" as I like to call them. I'd be lying if I said that I didn't still occasionally get freaked out when my heart rate is elevated unnecessarily. But at the time, it was far worse. To date, that has been the only occasion in which I had two episodes in one day.

After we got back downstairs, I texted my mom and told her what was going on. She instructed me to take one of my Xanax just to make it through the remainder of the volunteer time and told me my dad would meet me at my house when I was done to make sure I was feeling alright. I'm sure she already knew that I'd really just worked myself up into a panic attack and that it had nothing to do with my physical health whatsoever.

By the time volunteering was over, I was very on edge and happy to be on the way home. I felt so disappointed that whatever had happened impacted my volunteer experience this time around. Because of what happened, I also decided to skip my work's

Christmas party that evening. The day was turning out to be a real bummer. At least I had my dad's visit to look forward to when I got home.

Once he arrived, I asked if he would stay the night since I was feeling shaky. Being the amazing dad he is, of course he said yes. He needed to run some errands, so we went to the mall so he could go to the Apple store and then grabbed dinner. The rest of the night, we relaxed and watched tv until we went to bed. The next day I woke up feeling fine and went about my day as planned.

A week later, I was in an Orangetheory class and the whole experience happened again. I wish I could really explain what it feels like when it comes on. My whole body just starts to get hot and tingly and then my heart rate shoots up super high. I was in my floor block, which if you've never been to OT is the block where you're using weights/doing ab work/maybe doing some HIIT cardio and was actually on one of our breaks between blocks.

I looked up at the TV screen that shows everyone's performance and saw that my heart rate had shot up to around 170 bpm. Now, of course it was already elevated because I was working out but should have been nowhere near that level. Just like in the volunteer scenario, I walked out of the studio and sat on the bench, trying not to make a big deal of it. The head trainer happened to be in the studio before the next class was due to start, and he sat with me to make sure I was ok. I played it off and told him that it had happened before, and I was fine.

After a few minutes, my heart rate started to come down just a bit and so I tried to go back in and finish my workout. I was ok for about five minutes before it shot up again. At this point, the class was nearly over so I just went home. I remained calm for the most part, but after getting out of the shower I had a full-on meltdown. I texted my mom freaking out, and she offered to come over and drive me to work to make sure I was ok.

While I waited for her to arrive, I called my cardiologists office and told them what was going on. I was due for my six-month follow up anyway, so the nurse said she'd try to get me in that week. While I was at work, they called and said they were going to put me back on a heart monitor for two weeks, but this time it would be continually monitoring 24 hours a day instead of just monitoring for unusual heartbeat patterns.

I was almost relieved to get the monitor. They were able to get me in around 2pm that day to fit me for the monitor and get it attached. I would wear the monitor continuously for two weeks and then submit the data for results. Once the results came in, my cardiologist would evaluate them and call me back for a follow up. In the meantime, I was to go about business as usual so he could get an accurate depiction of day-to-day life. Remember when I told you that the obsession with the heart issue never really went away? Yeah, here ya go. Back at it again. (But, I promise, after this I do try harder.)

While I was on the monitor, I tried to identify variables that may have contributed to the resurgence of heart palpitations and anxiety. The only true identifiable change in my life over the last few months were the vitamins I began taking in since August. Not really considering possible consequences, I decided to cold-turkey completely stop taking them. Mind you, all this heart monitor/heart palpitation/anxiety/vitamin stopping business was over the Christmas holiday. It was not my brightest idea by far.

When I made the foolish decision to stop taking the vitamins, I was convinced they were the culprit, not remembering that they were brain altering vitamins. As you can see, I spent (*cough* spend *cough*) a great deal of time trying to identify what outside forces were affecting my mental and physical health instead of looking inside and realizing I was the problem, but more on that later.

The consequences of discontinuing all use of the vitamins was detrimental. After a few days, withdrawal symptoms set in. My anxiety had skyrocketed. I couldn't sleep, felt constantly agitated, had horrific mood swings, and felt out of control. The first few days were manageable, but after about a week, I was in shambles. Still to this day, I feel like I ruined my brother's Christmas visit, because for a good part of it, I was in a state of disarray.

This all turned into a gargantuan nightmare. The week before

Christmas, I brought my kitty and some clothes over to my parents with the intention of staying there for a week and enjoying the holidays with family. I wouldn't end up leaving for over three months.

I thanked my lucky stars that I was on PTO at the time and wouldn't have to go back to work for nearly two weeks. Like I said, after about a week, I felt like a dumpster fire. I made an appointment with my GP to give anxiety medication a second go, because I was desperate.

My GP is the sweetest doctor you could imagine, so she was wanting to get me back in action as soon as possible. She started me off on a 5mg dose of Lexapro, which is below the lowest therapeutic dose. We were to give this a try for a few a week or two and see how I progressed. In the meantime, she advised I find a psychiatrist, as they would be able to provide a level of care beyond her capabilities. She also recommended I stay with my parents for the time being, because of what happened last time with the suicidal ideations.

Lexapro is one of the most commonly prescribed anti-anxiety medications, so I was hopeful. But yet again, I let my desperation get the best of me. You might be screaming at me in your head right now "CARRIE! What about the vitamins? Couldn't they interact with the medication?" If you are, you've hit the nail on the head. The vitamins contained a significant dose of 5-HTP, which I would need to flush out of my system before even entertaining prescription meds, which meant weeks of waiting. I did not realize this at the time, so starting the Lexapro actually made my situation tank even further.

After a few days, I stopped the medication completely. I stopped everything completely actually. No vitamins, no medication, no energy drinks, no coffee, no alcohol. Oh yeah, and barely any food. My anxiety and agitation were so bad that I had zero appetite. The only food I had a taste for were my mom's famous kiffles. If you don't know what they are, they're these delicious little cookies made with hand rolled pastry, filled with a homemade walnut paste, and topped with powdered sugar. And shout out to my mom who had an entire Tupperware container full of them.

Because of my lack of appetite, I lost seven pounds in a little over a week and wouldn't gain it back for a while. For someone who is extremely active and works out almost every day, I'm always trying to lose a few pounds. Especially because my lust for peanut butter and ice cream may be a little out of control, but I digress. Losing those pounds was not worth it. I would take them back and then some to never have to go through that harrowing experience again.

I was on 24/7 high alert and could not stand to be in my own body. It was like riding a wave during a bad thunderstorm. There were brief moments of sanity where I thought I had seen the worst of it but would be quickly proven wrong. On top of the mental portion of this, my heart rate was still soaring all day every day. This had a colossal effect on one significant portion of my life, the one that keeps me grounded, allows me to alleviate stress and gives me a sense of control... my workouts.

Remember when reading this that I had a ridiculous fascination with my heart rate. So, normally during a high impact workout, think Orangetheory or spinning, I would peak out around 160-170 bpm. Lifting weights and light HIIT training got me around 120-150 and walking around 90-110. I only know all this, because I use my Apple Watch to track my workouts and the data is provided with each workout. I didn't look into any of this until my heart rate was jumping into the 140s when I was walking or 170's when I was lifting weights.

It freaked me out big time. I can't even lie. During this period of time (December 2019 - February 2020), I kept up with my workouts, but they were no longer enjoyable. Skipping them would've affected my mental state even further, so I pressed on despite how I felt. I started having my dad come with me. I would refuse to go to the gym without him because I was too afraid. What if something happened to me while I was there alone? What if I couldn't contact someone? What if I was in there with other people, and I had a full-blown panic attack? Panic attacks DID happen while we were there, but at least he was there to calm me down and bring me home.

Daily workouts with dad would remain a thing for the duration of my 3 ½ month stay. In fact, having a parent at every life activity was pretty much the norm from the beginning. Have you ever had to crawl in the bed with your mother in the middle of the night at 33 years old? I can tell you it's just as uncool and undesirable at 33 as it is at 3, but at the time it felt safe. It got old after a week, because mom snored (sorry, Mom hehe) and the litter box was in the far corner of their bedroom near the screened in porch. Mom's cat, Atticus, has the most putrid smelling poop, which he likes to leave daily around 5pm, and it was disturbing what little sleep I was getting.

The week I stayed in bed with mom was right after Christmas. While my brother was still visiting, we went to the mall for a little post-Christmas shopping. I wanted to try a weighted blanket because I'd gotten rave reviews from friends on the effectiveness and felt it was time I had my own. That blanket ended up being an incredible investment. I became a modern-day adult woman version of Linus from Charlie Brown. I drug that thing into mom's room every night in an attempt to get some sleep or feel some comfort. And by the way, I still use it every night to sleep.

I was also using my Xanax to try to sleep. This would carry on for a month. My GP told me I could take up to three a night, so that's what I did. I tried different combinations every night. 1 when I went to bed, 2 when I woke up. 2 when I went to bed, 1 when I woke up. 1 when I went to bed, 1 when I woke up (twice). This would help for an hour at a time, but inevitably, I'd wake up feeling the dark, cold, creeping anxiety feelings I felt every single night.

During some of the really bad episodes, mom would wake up too and hold me in her arms, rub my arm, stroke my hair and do whatever she could to make me feel better. Eventually, I would lull back to sleep. One of the sweeter moments during these nights with mom was my sweet baby boy. Since I adopted him, he has slept with me every single night. This didn't stop while I was in mom's bed. He would seek me out in the darkness and come snuggle up with us, which always brought a tiny moment of joy to mom and myself.

I haven't even gotten to the real sleep related bonus yet! Every. Single. Day. And I mean, every day (dad, you can fact check me), I woke up anywhere between 3am and 5am with a sense of dread I cannot put into words. Staying in my bed was not an option. The overwhelming fear and agitation drove me out of bed nearly every time. For months, this would be the norm. This crap was like living with a little, angry demon controlling my brain.

By this point, my dad was on the second floor, sleeping on the couch, his "lair" as mom and I call it. He would creep down during the night and check on me and constantly had his ear to the ground in case I woke up in a panic. This poor man probably slept as little as I did for the duration of my stay as a result.

Now back to my demon brain's early morning routine. When the catastrophic "world is ending-- someone is going to kidnap and kill my family-- I'm about to get murdered" feeling would arrive each day before daybreak, I would haul my blanket through the dark, down the hallway, up the stairs and curl up in the big squishy green chair in dad's lair, where he would be awaiting my arrival.

Some days I would curl up on the chair and wait for the feeling to pass, gently dozing off for an additional hour or two before our daily morning workout. Other days, when it was all too much to handle anymore, I would go upstairs and cry. My parents would be rolling in the dough if they had a dollar for every time I asked, "Will this ever get better?" "Will the medicine ever work?" "Will I ever go back to normal?" In the morning, those words would frequently be accompanied by giant, hot tears, and lots of pain.

I was so scared. Petrified. What happened to me? What did I do to myself? I would ask myself these questions so many times over the next few months, but they always hit hardest first thing in the morning when the fear and adrenaline peaked.

Dad and I continued this morning tradition for months, even when I went back to work. That was the worst. I would crawl up there before work and dad would bring me some Pedialyte, ginger ale, or water and I would sit there until, by some grace of God, I would fall back to sleep. Mom would always come and check on me the moment she was awake. I think she probably stopped checking my bed to see if I was there and just trekked up the stairs to my big green chair to see what state I was in. Eventually I'd give up on sleep, and dad and I would begin the second part of the morning at the gym. The routine got old really quick, I tell ya. Being deliriously exhausted every day was miserable, but I'm damn lucky to have the parents I do.

There have been times recently when I have meditated and the vision that pops up is me, sitting in that chair sobbing and wondering when I would feel human again. That vision has brought me to tears. I want to reach out to old me, wrap her in my arms and tell her it'll all be ok. I want to give her hope and make her feel safe. It breaks my own heart to see myself like that.

It was like regressing back into childhood. Like I said, I didn't and couldn't do anything alone. Eat, sleep, walk, workout, go to the store, drive to work, etc. Next to working out and sleeping, driving was my least favorite. With the unpredictability of the attacks my brain chemicals were waging, I didn't dare take to the roads alone. During the two weeks I was home on PTO, this was perfectly fine.

When I stay with my parents, I generally ride with them when we leave the house anyways, but when I had to go back to the office, it wasn't ideal. I was praying to the Lord above, and any other higher power, that by the time I had to go back to the office, this would all be a thing of the past. WRONG! At least my boss, the most understanding and compassionate human, let me work from home on the last few days before I was due back after the New Year's holiday. I used this time in the privacy of my parent's home, to call our Employee Assistance Program and find a psychiatrist to help me sort out the mess I'd gotten into, hoping to be seen the following week. I couldn't get an appointment for three weeks, so I would have to carry on until then.

I had to return to work the week of January 6th. One of my biggest fears during this time was losing my job, and I had no intention of letting that happen. I was nervous, but mom thought it'd be good for me to get out of the house and pour my energy into something productive. She was right to an extent. Work gave me a sense of purpose and distracted me from the usual litany of horrors I had going on inside my head. However, there was that whole detail of getting there.

You guessed it, mom or dad drove me every day. They dropped me off and picked me up. Some days there were panic attacks or meltdowns on the way. Most days, I would just sit in silence, dreaming of when they would come back to pick me up and I could head back to the couch with my weighted blanket and hibernate away from the rest of society. That is just what I did every day for the first few months of 2020: Come home from work, change into pajamas and crawl under my weighted blanket. The only time I came out from under that guy was to get my food and go to the bathroom. I missed my walks listening to My Favorite Murder, but murder podcasts weren't the best when your head was already full of self-inflicted horrors. I also missed reading. Books are my passion, and I am a reading machine, but during that time, I felt so out of my mind that I couldn't focus enough to make it through a page. It was weighted blanket and TV time only, with absolutely ZERO news, because it triggered my anxiety.

At some point in the first few weeks back, I made a promise to myself that I would drive myself to work as a birthday gift to myself. That was going to be the first major step I took towards getting back to a "normal" life, as I called it. I said that a lot during that time. "When will I ever feel normal again?" "I just want to be normal." I learned after a while that there is no "normal." No one is "normal" we just operate on a personal sliding scale of complete glee and dark insanity.

Anyway, the month passed by, and I got to the week of my birthday. A few notable events occurred that week. First, I drove my ass to work. Go me! That felt scary, but also pretty good. Secondly, like I mentioned before, Brad and I had randomly connected for a period of time after the breakup. At one point, we even entertained him coming for a visit for the holidays like we had previously planned. He messaged me on Christmas and sent well wishes to the family, and also texted me on New Year's Day to tell me he was in a funk and missed me. Yada, yada, yada.

He texted me the week of my birthday, knowing good and well that it was the week of my birthday, I was less than a month into overcoming a full-on mental breakdown. He also knew that I had trouble getting over the breakup but had the audacity to tell me that he was seeing someone new. I asked whether he really thought it was a good time to tell me something like that, knowing what I was going through. He only said that he had held off as long as he could because he had already been seeing her for a while.

Hmmm... a while, eh?! Barely three weeks had gone by since he had told me he was lonely and missed me. Although I was over it when I received the message I almost threw up. Why did he have to tell me in the first place? I feel like part of it might have been guilt he was harboring for still talking to me while he was dating her, but I'll never know that to be a fact. During the conversation he said that he still wanted to be friends because I will always be an important part of his life and he will always have love for me. I was kind of being a bitch back and told him I wasn't sure, basically responding to all following texts with "ok." I let it rest for the remainder of the day, because I was hurt and wasn't really sure how to respond.

The next day I texted him and basically told him it was fine. I also told him that at some point in the future, perhaps we could be friends. He expressed that he felt like I should be happy for him because he deserved it. Something about he deserved to find someone he can be with and develop a relationship and love. Yeah, our situation wasn't ideal by any means, but this broke my heart. The way he said all of that cut deep. I'm so used to being easily replaced by men that this just kind of touched a nerve somewhere. After this conversation we wouldn't speak again for a long time.

I was hoping after that news, which I didn't even want to share with my friends since they all thought he was great, I thought maybe my birthday week would perk up a bit. Welp, not so much. I had been wanting to do a Chakti yoga birthday party for so long. It was the ultimate way to celebrate. If you've never been to Chakti, it's a combination of twerking and yoga. You let loose, free your spirit, allow your true self to shine through and just have an incredible time in a loving, accepting, judgement free zone.

I had booked the birthday party months earlier and given the yoga instructor a down payment. Obviously, when I booked the party, I wasn't expecting to have such a dramatic shift in life circumstances. The week of the party, I was putting a lot of pressure on myself to be able to go. I already had a Facebook invitation out with tons of girlfriends invited and messaged some others to add on last minute. Throughout the week, I was feeling marginally better, but by the weekend I had worried myself into a frenzy.

The entire day and night before the party's expected date, I was freaking out. What the heck would I do if I had a panic attack during class? I was still having unusual spikes in heart rate when I worked out, and Chakti really got you sweating. I texted Lynny and she promised me I'd be fine and that she'd be there with me and would take me and leave if I started feeling uncomfortable. That was comforting until I started making up all types of scenarios that could possibly happen.

What if I have a major panic attack or another episode of SVT, and I have to leave and go sit out in the hall? Everyone will be worried, and the class will have to stop, and it'll be a big waste of everyone's time. Then everyone will think I'm dramatic or feel inconvenienced for even showing up. And what if it's even worse than that and one of my parents has to come get me? Someone will have to sit and wait with me for an hour while they drive from South Carolina, and that will be so embarrassing, and I just can't stand to have that happen. You can start to see how I was making myself nuts over this.

All of these ruminations sent me down a dark spiral. I could not sleep the night before and woke up with one of my epic 5am panic attacks. I ended up on my dad's couch in the lair and was sobbing hysterically. I couldn't go through with the party. I ruined my own birthday. I had to message so many girls to tell them I wasn't having my party anymore. Around 8am, I messaged the instructor to tell her what was going on and cancel the party. I felt awful because she had been planning on hosting the class and had already put a deposit down on the space. Then I went ahead and texted all of my friends. What a mess! I was devastated and it was all my own doing.

Of course, a few hours later I completely regretted canceling. There was no going back at this point. I had already told people it was canceled and wasn't going to play that game. Not to mention, some of the girls were driving 90 minutes just to get there. Yikes. This is where things look up just a bit.

My core group of friends is a bunch of absolute unicorns. I don't deserve these humans at all. They were bound and determined to get me out of the house and help me celebrate my day. Bria, Lynn, Jen, and Megan got together and made reservations for a birthday lunch at Leroy Fox in Southend, a company where some of us used to work. Chelsea and Kelsey drove an hour and a half to come to lunch, even though my party was canceled. Dad drove me since I was in a state of disarray but insisted on just dropping me off so I could spend time with my friends since the only people I ever saw were him and my mom.

It was the best couple of hours I had in months. I got to see my friends and hug them and catch up. What a blessing! They were so sweet and brought me gifts and cards and gave me that "normal" feeling I had been looking for. They didn't treat me like I was a burden or act as if something were wrong with me. They supported me and loved me even when I was at my lowest point. That was the best birthday gift I could have ever received. True love, support, kindness, and friendship when I had little to offer in return. That crappy day turned into something really special, and I will truly never forget all these girls have done for me.

After the birthday weekend drama, it was finally time for my first psychiatrist appointment. I think this would be a good point in the story to break into the uncertainties that are psychiatrists and anxiety meds.

ANXIETY MEDS:
THE SHIT NO ONE TELLS YOU

On January 28, 2020, I had my first appointment with a psychiatrist. Because of my first experience with anxiety medication, I was not keen on trying the medication route again. On my first go around with medication, I had this fantastical idea that anxiety medication would solve my whole problem. Pop a pill and voila! I'm cured. No more panic attacks, no more waking up with feelings of dread, no more getting stressed at work and no more anxiousness when going about everyday activities.

I thought that with one simple pill, I was going to I was going to wake up feeling like a billion dollars every day, carefree and excited for what the day had in store. Nah, folks. That is 100% not how it works. Looking back, I probably should have done this whole psychiatrist thing sooner. My lack of knowledge about the anxiety medication process, because yes, it is a process, lead to a lot of my fear. No one had given me the gruesome details about what the process involved or what types of side effects I might experience during my first experience with medication. Now that I was going to see someone who specializes in this area, I was going into round two better informed.

When I started to explore the idea of finding a psychiatrist, I called into the Employee Assistance Program (EAP) hotline offered through work. After giving some details about my situation and immediate needs, the EAP contact sent over a long list of providers covered by our insurance. I spent some time going through the list, which had over a hundred names. I googled some of the practitioners listed. Eastover Psychological and Psychiatric Group had excellent ratings, as did most of their practitioners, but they did not accept my insurance, so I ended up at Atrium Behavioral Health.

I was matched with Aislinn and was both nervous and excited to meet her. First, they asked me to provide a urine sample. I was like, "Huh? I'm just here for a medication consultation", but I guess this is standard to make sure you're not abusing illegal drugs. Then they check your weight to make sure it's not fluctuating too dramatically. Now on to the interrogation: Have you wanted to harm yourself or others? Have you attempted to harm yourself? Are you having suicidal thoughts? Have you used any illegal substances or alcohol? Why are you here today? No matter how many times I visit her, these questions still give me the heebeegeebees.

I was then sent to another waiting room, back in the secure part of the basement floor where all the offices are located. After another 10-15 minutes, Aislinn calls me back. She's not what I expected from a psychiatric nurse practitioner, although I guess I didn't have any prior experience for comparison. She almost reminded me of an elementary school teacher, kind of quirky, very energetic, glasses, talkative and to the point. I wasn't sure what to make of her yet, but we would have an hour to get to know one another.

Once we started talking, I explain what I have going on. She quickly narrows in on generalized anxiety disorder and tries to decide if we have to contend with any traces of bipolar, which is quickly ruled out. Now we get into the medication portion. Since my first experience with meds was so troubling, I was apprehensive to try again and was hoping she would change my mind. After receiving the appointment confirmation, I had googled her and was relieved to find that she did have some five-star reviews.

Once we have gotten past the metal detectors and psych ER, we are instructed to go down to the basement. This is the location of the clinical offices. Picture fluorescent lights, that cream/tan tile from your elementary school lunchroom, old, bonded leather chairs, and a tiny TV.

I go check in and then sit down and wait. After about 15 minutes, I'm called back. I give a brief overview of my experience with Zoloft, what dosage my GP started with, how we increased, what happened while I was taking it, etc. Like I said before, I ended up feeling ten times worse and had suicidal ideations. But with the Zoloft, my dosage was increased very quickly. Every few days, I had to take a bit more until reaching the ideal therapeutic dosage. This method doesn't work for everyone.

Aislinn was the first person to give me some kind of education on medication. The primary thing I learned is that it's a trial-and-error process. Because numerous options are available, your practitioner makes an educated guess as to which one will be most suitable for your particular troubles. Do you have bipolar, manic depression, generalized anxiety, OCD, PTSD or social anxiety? Is it a combination of a few? Figuring that out helps to narrow down which medications to try first.

Don't get discouraged during this part of the process. Because there is no testing to determine the proper medication per person or other clean-cut means of identifying what will work best, the process can be frustrating. The average number of medication dosage/type changes is thirteen before you find what works. You also have to wait between four to eight weeks to see if what was prescribed is actually effective or not, because it has to work its way into your system. If you have gone through this process, I applaud you. It's not easy and you are strong beyond your knowledge, but you also probably know that it is worth the patience. Mine would certainly be tested through this process, as you will see.

Another complexity is that most medication is prescribed to treat more than one type of issue. For example, I'm on Lexapro now, which is an SSRI, or Selective Serotonin Reuptake Inhibitor. It's also considered an antidepressant used also to treat anxiety. And it doesn't stop there. After a few months, you may discover you need a second medication to kind of "boost" the first one. This was the case for me. In addition to Lexapro, I also take Lamictal, which is an epilepsy medication used as a mood stabilizer.

All of this contributes to why I have wanted to live a medication free life. It was a confusing process for me and the practitioner. Each patient is different, so each patient may need any combination of meds. Luckily, there is a small base of widely tolerated drugs that are a good starting point. Lexapro is one of those.

Aislinn suggested the Lexapro to me, which is what I had tried with my GP just a month earlier. She said I may have had such an adverse reaction, because the vitamins were still in my system and needed to clear out. I was willing to give it another shot. She planned to slowly progress my dosage. I would be starting at 5mg for a few weeks, then onto 10mg, then I would come back for a revisit.

She also showed me the equivalent of a clinical medication encyclopedia that described the therapeutic dosages, the side effects, what the medication was used for, etc. This gave me some confidence to try the medication again. The part I still didn't know was just how long it was going to take to work.

Some of my friends said their medication started working right away. Some of them started on 5mg and some went right to 10mg. Some were sleeping better right away, and my friend Connie described it as "living her best life." I had high hopes, but everyone is different. I'm of course, one of the difficult ones.

My anxiety and agitation spiked right away, and my sleeping hadn't improved. By the way, at this point in my mental breakdown journey, I hadn't slept soundly in a month. It was really starting to wear on me. How was I supposed to battle this anxiety and work towards recovery when I could barely keep my eyes open? Lack of sleep can aggravate mental illness and normal day to day emotion. And it was busy season at work. Can't forget that. Every day was just a battle until I could get back to bed. That's when round two of the battle would begin, while I laid tossing and turning, depending solely on my Xanax to try to get a few hours' sleep.

After giving the Lexapro about a week to help with the sleep issue, I sent Aislinn a message that it hadn't improved. This angel of a human then sent me Trazodone. This is another SSRI and not all SSRI's are made alike. Trazodone used to be prescribed to treat anxiety but is now used more like a sedative. I was nervous to add in another SSRI, but the pharmacist reassured my dad and myself that Lexapro and Trazodone was a common combo.

I thank the Lord above for the medication. Half a tablet was 50mg. I was dead in my bed within 15 minutes and slept like a rock. Now it didn't quite work that well after the first night, but damn, I needed that sleep. I woke up feeling like a new person the next day and ready to take on the world.

Over the following weeks, I would experience a variety of symptoms. Sometimes I'd feel really wired, sometimes agitated, sometimes SUPER high and happy, sometimes really dark. It varied from day to day. I think the worst was in the first couple of weeks when I was feeling extremely agitated. I was eating dinner on the couch and my sweet boy kitten started to beg for my food. I got so mad. I wanted to scream at him and tell him to get away.

This broke my heart into a thousand pieces. I never wanted to feel that way again. He is my entire heart and soul and the one thing that has kept me sane through all of this, and there I was, being an ungrateful little bitch to him. What kind of mother was I? I cannot imagine experiencing this with a real child. I sobbed about it in therapy that week and tried to remind myself that it was part of the medication process, not my actual feelings.

Life would continue to be a mental health rollercoaster for months. Every time the dosage changed, or a new medication was added, I had to wait six to eight WEEKS to evaluate the full effects of the medication or change. That applied when the dosage increased as well. The first couple of increases were administered within four weeks because I was in dire need of a higher dose, but dang.

This shit sucked. One of my best friends from college, Clarisse, who is a nurse practitioner, was starting to feel really bad for me. It didn't take this long for everyone to start to see steady improvement externally, but for some reason, my brain was on the slow track. From the beginning she thought I would need to go up to the max dose, which is 20mg. I hated the thought of that. Why couldn't I be like most people and hang out around 10mg? There would be no more increases available if I hit 20mg, and what if my anxiety refused to cooperate?

I was annoyed and, at many points, terrified I'd have to go through this entire process again with a new medication. After a few months, I was becoming open to the option because I wanted to feel better so badly. But I kept up with the increases. At some point I finally reached 20mg, yet still wasn't feeling like a million bucks. Aislinn suggested we add Lamictal before completely switching medications to see how it would go. The combination still isn't perfect, but it'll have to do for now.

I had no clue what I had gotten myself into. Clarisse and my girl, Adasha, were always available for questions, encouragement, words of advice and personal experience to help soothe my worries. Aislinn also made herself as available as possible. Atrium has a message portal where you can send emails to your doctor, and I used this when I wasn't sure what else to do. Aislinn or one of her colleagues, always responded promptly and tried to provide reassurance.

This was all the crap no one had warned me about. It could be as easy as a few weeks or a year long journey to see if a specific medication or combination of medications will work for you. If it didn't, you get to repeat the process with a new medication. But you have to stay strong and remind yourself, that going through the process again, or maybe a few more times, MIGHT help you find something that works for you.

Dammit! Why is this process so difficult?! I told myself multiple times that I wouldn't wish it on my worst enemy. It's an arduous task to hold it together some days. In fact, some people have to take FMLA or medical leave just to make it through the process. Take that into account, I guess my experience wasn't all that bad, but it wasn't fun.

The 5am visits to my dad's lair, full of tears and terror that I'd never feel better still existed. I was still tired at work but was doing my best to push through. At the very least, my heart rate was starting to normalize. Aislinn had told me it was going so crazy because my cortisol levels were too high. A few weeks on the medication should do the trick. And bless it, she was right. At least my workouts were becoming enjoyable again, and I could work towards going back to classes.

Phase one of this medication journey lasted about four months and phase two is ongoing. My suggestion to anyone wanting to give medication a try is to educate yourself. Look into potential side effects. Now don't go all WebMD on me because you'll scare yourself. A basic medication search will give you the top common side effects experienced with each medication. Also, remember some side effects are transient. That means that they may only last the first week or two when beginning a medication and each dosage/medication change. I did experience these. There were peaks in discomfort levels and additional anxiety/agitation, but that never lasted long. After a while, everything will stabilize, and you can better judge how you're reacting to the med.

Try to stay optimistic and open. Stay open to trying new things and stay open with your provider. They cannot help you if you aren't honest, so keep an open line of communication. If they aren't willing to have this level of communication and do not give you the attention you deserve, FIND SOMEONE ELSE. There are just as many good psychiatric practitioners out there as careless ones. Some are just there to collect a paycheck, so find one that has empathy, compassion, knowledge, and experience.

Talk to friends, loved ones or people you trust who have used medication before. Your experience may vary widely from theirs, but it may at least give you some perspective to get started. After talking to friends, I was able to bring medication options to Aislinn and discuss them with her. And if it weren't for my incredible massage therapist, Jess, I would've never known we could add a second medication to boost Lexapro before switching to something new. The information she provided ended up being beneficial at my next appointment.

My best advice is this: DO NOT USE GOOGLE. Don't google and read people's reviews on medication. I did this far too often and added to my own agony. It's not worth it. Remember that people typically write reviews when they are unhappy, so don't trust everything you read. Your experience belongs to you and you only and so does theirs. You could miss out on the perfect treatment if you stay wrapped up in what strangers are doing.

I'm hoping to not be on my medications for the rest of my life, but the future is unpredictable. I no longer look at them as a crutch, but as a helpful friend that gets me through the day to day. Are they perfect? No. I still wake up anxious many days and experience bad anxiety every few weeks, but that's part of the process. The medications aren't a miracle worker. They're a helping hand to get you on your feet, so that you're able to do the work needed to heal yourself, i.e., therapy. Regardless of your decision to either try or avoid medication altogether, don't give up and keep pushing on, because with determination and hard work, anything is possible.

The most interesting part of writing a book about your own life experiences is that they really never stop happening and can give you some interesting turn of events to talk about. I made it through summer doing ok with my meds and living life as normally as possible. I mean as normally as you can live during a worldwide pandemic. Once fall hit, the seasonal depression started to kick in. I had never realized that I had Seasonal Affective Disorder before, but it's amazing what you can learn when you are trapped with yourself daily. Well, maybe your pet, but they can't exactly talk to you.

At first, I wasn't really concerned, but after a few weeks of not wanting to get out of bed, workout, work, go on walks or see my friends, I decided to contact Aislinn via our online portal. She decided we needed to throw another medication into the mix. I had my maxed-out dose of Lexapro for anxiety, Lamictal to keep me leveled out and now I got to add a very low dose of Wellbutrin for a little dopamine booster. While I wanted a remedy to the issue, I can't say I was excited about the game plan.

As you already know, I wanted no parts of medications to begin with, and now I was going to be on three. On top of that, I had finally gotten past all the terrible side effects of the other medications, and I just wasn't mentally ready to do it again. I was apprehensive to start, so I waited until the weekend had passed and decided on the following Monday.

I don't know why I continue to do this to myself, but we were in busy season again when I was due to start this new med. It was quite possibly the worst one I've ever worked in all three years at my job. The first few days went by smoothly, aside from feeling hyped up on caffeine, except it wasn't caffeine. It was the meds. Then it went downhill for a bit. I felt insane. I was anxious and crying and not sleeping great. Oh, and then there's the stuff you don't want to think about…I also couldn't go to the bathroom, so I felt like a whale. The whole situation was quite unpleasant.

Fast forward a week or two later, the side effects are starting to fade, and I started to feel more energized. This medicine thing, man I tell ya, it's something else. You have to pay attention to your body and how you feel and continue to be transparent with your provider when circumstances change. Something that may have been working for a while may begin to require adjustments, additions, or complete changes. The only people that can make that determination is you and your provider.

My biggest point of this is to remind you to be openminded and accepting of change. The changes you are resisting may be the very ones that turn everything around. Now back to the good stuff.

2020:
NO ONE WAS EXPECTING THAT

After my birthday weekend had passed, we were full steam ahead in busy season. I know, it sounds like we have been in busy season forever, but really, year-end reporting season is the longest. Peak typically lasts about three to four weeks, but at year end, it drags on from January through March, with the worst of it in February.

I actually quite enjoy the peaks at work, because the days fly by, filled to the brim with meetings and meaningful tasks. Early 2020, it was almost necessary to my recovery. The work environment had improved dramatically. My coworker was being so kind to me, and I was beyond grateful. They were back to being the person I met when I first started, and it made a world of difference in the office. That reporting season had been a great learning opportunity for me, as it would be my first quarter working on my new, more challenging assignments, and they were an indispensable mentor. Working with them closely all quarter was extremely rewarding.

With the continued learning opportunities, I kept busy. Work was giving me a sense of purpose that disappeared the moment I stepped foot in the car to go home. For some reason, I was able to leave most of my anxiety issues at the security desk when I entered the door. Had I kept all of my business about my mental breakdown/anxiety med/living with my parents nonsense to myself, I really don't think anyone would've ever known. I think this is the beginning of where I started to be more open and transparent with my internal battle and am extremely grateful for the love and support I received from my entire team.

Perfection in life does not exist, so there were tough days. Our new staff provided a level of kindness and help that I'm extremely grateful for. Men like him do not exist in the sphere of life I occupy, other than my dad and brother. He was patient and so sweet to me. He would drive me to pick up my lunch or take me to Target, especially when my parents were still driving me to work. He would walk to get water with me or go on walks outside when I really needed a breath of fresh air.

When the crazy ups and downs of the medicine were affecting me and I couldn't leave my desk, I would Skype him and he would provide encouragement. The amount of times he told me that he knew everything would get better, I can't count 'em. How does someone so young have so much empathy and compassion, especially a man?! I do not know, but he will always have a place in my heart for his support and friendship. My parents too because he became a fan fav amongst the family. This may also be why I always bake him so many cookies.

Two of my favorite mangers also stood by my side through this process, and while it might have been an awkward thing to handle someone's personal life, they really excelled. I felt as if I could be open with them about what was going on at home, which made me feel more relaxed at work. Some other coworkers served as a sounding board, and their support meant more than they really knew.

Work was keeping me preoccupied, but the results of my heart rate monitor were constantly nagging in the back of my head. Why had they not called yet with the results? At some point, I finally took it upon myself to call and get an update from the nurse. Apparently, the monitor results came back normal, so they felt no need to contact me. Receiving a positive update on my testing was great and all, but I assumed they would have scheduled a face to face with the cardiologist to deliver the news. So, I weaseled my way into an appointment to talk to him in person.

My cardiologist is an odd fellow and sometimes makes me uneasy. He comes highly rated and is one of the best in his craft, so I trust his expertise, but he can be quite off-putting. On this specific visit, he explained that I was fine and not showing signs of irregular heart rhythms. Then he went into a diatribe about my stress and anxiety.

This man told me that if I believed in God, prayed, and put all my trust in him that my anxiety would all go away. First, I think it's presumptuous of him to assume that all of his patients are Believers. I don't think there's anything wrong with him discussing faith and an alternative means of "healing", but I think it's unprofessional to assume everyone shares your beliefs. Secondly, mental health disorders don't just "go away." Lastly, he told me that people aren't born needing Xanax and Lexapro, so I shouldn't need them to feel better.

Man, I was not in the mood for him. I had already beat myself up enough about getting on medication and dealing with anxiety issues, but how dare he throw that in my face? I did not come to your office for you to advise me on the state of my mental health, which is none of your damn business. Thankfully, my dad had come along for this visit because he talked me off the ledge on the way to the car. But I'll count my blessings. My heart is strong and working properly, so I can avoid seeing this guy for the foreseeable future.

After tackling the majority of busy season and getting positive heart monitor results, I was about to get the most unwelcome surprise. One Sunday night, my parents and I were hanging out at home, per usual. I think I was probably eating some Ben & Jerry's out of the carton, because ... who doesn't do that?! Mom came over to me and said, "I have to tell you something, but you can't get mad at me."

"Ok..." I responded.

Normally when she says that to me, she's going to tell me she bought me something or did something for me, which is sweet but also makes me uncomfortable because I don't want her wasting her money on me.

That wasn't it, but after she told me, oh how I wish it had been. She casually told me that during her last mammogram they found a lump. After a biopsy and some testing, the lump turned out to be cancerous. I was the last person they told because my mental state was still pretty fragile, and she didn't want me to worry. I was only a month into the medication and a long road to recovery still lay ahead. But at that moment, it was no longer about me.

The first few minutes after she told me, I felt like I turned to stone. This isn't the first time that I'd received shocking news and had a delayed emotional reaction. I guess it's just how my brain is wired. I seemed to be holding it together fine, but after a few minutes, I was sobbing. She wrapped me in her arms and told me that she planned to be around a long, long time to drive me crazy. She swore to me that it was going to be fine.

Regardless how many times they reassured me she was a best-case scenario, I was still deeply concerned. Based on the tests that were performed, they only found that one lump. The cancer didn't appear to have spread and hadn't affected her lymph nodes. If she had a lumpectomy and then a round of radiation, there was a 99% chance she'd go into remission forever. I was still distraught.

This was my mom. Nothing could take her from me. She was a pillar of support and strength in my life. How could something so vile have taken up space inside my strong, loving mother?! But cancer doesn't discriminate. It doesn't care if you're the scum of the earth or the saintliest human. It comes as it pleases and does whatever damage it sees fit. My mom was ready to kick its ass, and I was here for whatever she needed. At this point, I was just like, "Please, God, no more bad news."

We all had to put on our brave faces and maintain optimism about her recovery. Surgery would occur on March 11th, which was just a few weeks away, and it would be an outpatient surgery. The doctor performing the surgery was supposedly one of the best at her craft and gave my parents a sense of reassurance. If they trusted her, I did too.

Carrie Thompson

When I got into work the next day, I gave my boss the news and explained that I would need a few days off that second week in March. I didn't really want to talk about it to anyone, but obviously had to let her know. Unfortunately, she's well versed in having a parent struggling with cancer, so she was very understanding of our newfound family dilemma. She assured me that taking the time off would be no problem and she also offered to be a source of support and advice.

The strange thing about this situation was that I had some odd feeling something was going on with Mom. She kept telling me she was having appointments but wouldn't tell me the nature of them. It was always just, "Oh a checkup with Dr. Ward…" or "I just have to have a test done…" but I had a sixth sense that something was brewing. I hate that, in some sense, I turned out to be right.

Another oddity occurred when my dad surprised both mom and me with a visit from my brother around Valentine's Day. He told us that he had to go to Lowes, but when 9pm rolled around and he still wasn't home, we were wondering where the heck he went. I texted him, because I was about to go to bed, but a moment later he walked through the door.

A second later, in came my brother. I sat there in shock for a moment or two and mom literally lost it. She was sobbing hysterically for over ten minutes. I can't lie, I cried too and had to force myself to stop. My brother had been texting me to check in since he left after Christmas and seeing him was such a welcome distraction. However, I still didn't understand why my mom could not stop crying. It was strange to me, but whatever. All I remember now is her saying to me, "We both needed this so much, didn't we?!"

Later that day, I discovered that she found out about the lump and was going to have to get more testing done. It all made more sense then, why she needed him as much as I did. That weekend was something special. For some reason, the Universe decided to give me a break. I woke up with low grade anxiety and felt happy and energized. My anxiety greatly diminished in his company, and I was actually able to enjoy myself and be carefree for a weekend. His visit gave me the pick-me-up I needed in busy season and in life. I have to give dad credit, sometimes his surprises are the best!

Anywho, making it through that busy season was a big freaking deal in my opinion. After each quarter my magical unicorn of a boss had touchpoints with another staff and me to get our feedback on the quarter. During that feedback session, I told her I was proud of myself for continuing to provide the level of performance that's expected of me despite the obstacles in my personal life.

I suck at giving myself credit for any damn thing, but when I look back at this, I think it can be considered a little milestone. Those were a few months of bravery, where I fought through a sea of shit to get to the other side, and dang, it felt good. I pride myself on being a reliable employee and hard worker, so the fact that I didn't let that slip made me feel a little bit like a boss.

When you're on the rockier roads of this journey called life, try to find ways to give yourself credit where credit is due. Honestly, for some people, this might be getting out of bed or taking a shower or making themselves breakfast. And if that sounds like you, hell yes, high five to you, badass! Progress typically comes in baby steps, not flying leaps, so recognize the small victories along the way. (By the way, I'm shit at taking my own advice here. I am the queen of instant gratification, so if this is you as well, I get it!)

As Q4 reporting season was coming to an end, COVID-19 was starting to make its appearance. I had a strict "no news show/news radio" rule with my family, so I rarely saw what was going on with current events. Hearing the turmoil going on in the world heightened my sense of foreboding, so I avoided it when possible. But this one did not escape me. Between the election and coronavirus, my rule was often violated.

To this day, I'm not sure our country was prepared for coronavirus to hit the states. The first reported death occurred in Seattle, WA near the end of February, but it would be a few weeks before Trump declared a state of emergency. By that point, a wave of panic rippled across the U.S., because there were so many unknowns. Anyone with anxiety knows, the more uncertain a situation, the more unnerving it becomes. Oh yeah, and the lack of control. How fun! You can take personal precautions, but you are at the mercy of the idiots around you to do the same. I think I remember asking God to leave me alone for a little while, but that wasn't in his master plan.

In the early stages, I didn't focus on coronavirus, because our family had bigger fish to fry. Mom's surgery was rapidly approaching and is a day I won't soon forget. The day of her surgery, she and my dad had to leave for the hospital around 6am. This would be the first morning I woke up alone, if you don't count the cats. I would have to go workout by myself, get my own coffee and breakfast and drive to the hospital by myself. I didn't have a clue where to park or go for her surgery.

If you're a parent, you probably relate to this better than I do, because most loving parents want nothing more than to fiercely protect their children. That being said, my mother was willing to drive herself to the hospital and go through all the pre-op steps alone, just so my dad could stay with me because I was scared. Of course, I refused. No matter what hurdles I'd have to jump that morning being alone, I was going to do it. I had put her through the parental ringer in the months prior, and I knew it ripped her heart to shreds to watch me suffer. That one day was not about to be centered around my temporary needs.

Mom also told me I didn't have to come to the hospital for her surgery. When she said that, I was more concerned about her sanity than her boob. The day of Mom's surgery was a day for me to be strong for both of us. She had put up the good fight for us both for long enough, and I wanted to give her my all that day.

Don't get excited and think that I pulled off this first day alone without a hitch. I still woke up with the crippling anxiety I'd become accustomed to but jumped my butt outta bed quickly and started the day. Distraction was always key. The first order of business was to decorate the kitchen for her return. The day before I'd gone to the Dollar Tree, which has the best budget décor ever. I grabbed some décor to welcome her home, even in her loopy post-op state. Next was the workout. Boom! Survived that one without any issues. Shower, breakfast, coffee, go!

Mom was going back to surgery at 9:30 AM, and my behind needed to arrive well in advance to see her off. Welp, Starbucks struck again, and I ended up late! Hospital parking is a royal pain in the you know where. My heart was going a mile a minute as I watched the minutes tick by. I took the first parking spot I saw and rushed inside, coffee splashing everywhere. When I get inside the building, I have no clue where to go. I frantically flagged down a nurse who was kind enough to point me in the direction of the elevator that could get me where I needed to go.

I was glad to have entered the building on the correct side because as soon as I exited the elevator, I was right near the surgical check-in desk. The kind older woman working the desk promptly asked how she could help. I explained my mom was there for surgery and would be going back soon but had no idea I was coming, and I needed to see her. That sweet lady handed me a visitor pass and had me swept away to the back as swiftly as possible.

This is my favorite part of the story and also the saddest. Right as we pass through the security doors to the surgery waiting rooms, my mom is being wheeled to surgery. The nurse is literally pushing her right towards me. All the emotion I held in for weeks since the news seeped out of me.

I called her name over and over, "Mom! Mom!" I had to hug her before she went back. She was drugged out of her mind but opened her eyes for a brief moment to give me a hug. I held her hand, and we both cried, but she was able to eventually get a laugh out of me. I looked up and the nurse pushing her had started crying, as did the ladies at the nurse's station. I might have been a little dramatic, but whatever. That's my mom. She's my whole world and my heart, and I just wanted her to be ok. A part of me feels like a higher being was with us that day. First and most importantly, mom's surgery went perfectly and second, she was delayed just a few minutes, which allowed me to see her in spite of my tardiness.

I feel kinda bad about the next part, because as soon as they wheeled her away from me, I walked back around the corner to find my dad and lost what little remaining composure I had. I mean, I was ugly crying. I collapsed into his arms and the dam broke. I probably scared the living heck out of everyone in the bays around us because of how hard I was crying.

After my meltdown, we headed to the waiting room for what would seem like a lifetime. I brought a book, but I don't think I read more than four or five pages. I killed time by perusing the gift shop and buying snacks I didn't need to eat. At one point, I had a mini panic attack, but talked myself off the ledge about 30 minutes later. The waiting was killing me.

There was a screen where you could track the progress of your patient, and Mom's name finally moved to the post-op status. While we waited for her sedation to wear off, we got to meet with the surgeon who gave us a stellar report on mom's condition. After we met with the surgeon, I thought we would get to see mom, but nope, more excruciatingly painful waiting.

A short while later, they finally led us back to her post-op bay. It was the big moment I'd been waiting for since arriving. Seeing her in pain and still groggy from the anesthesia broke my heart. I had never seen my brave, warrior momma in such a weakened state, which brought me to tears yet again. I held her hand, and we both cried, but she was able to eventually get a laugh out of me.

Apparently, she didn't fully remember seeing me before surgery. I guess she kind of thought I was like a mirage or a dream. While we were sitting in the bay with her, she asked me if she had seen me before surgery, which I quickly confirmed she had. She then proceeded to tell me that all she remembered was seeing a Starbucks cup. This at least gave me a chuckle.

After another hour or so had passed, we finally got to take her home, where she saw my decorations and laid down to sleep the rest of the day away. I was ecstatic that we had her home and could spend the rest of the day keeping an eye on her.

While we were waiting for her to get out of surgery, my coworker texted to inform me that we were going to be on work from home for at least two weeks and that they were making everyone pack up their belongings and leave the office. I did not believe him, because I would always joke how my favorite holiday was "early dismissal Friday" or "work from home Wednesday." After pretending to get offended that I didn't believe him, he sent me a photo of the company-wide email that was distributed, and he was most certainly telling the truth. Two employees from our office had been sent for COVID testing and until their test results returned, everyone had to work from home. In the meantime, the office would be deep cleaned and await our return. COVID was just becoming breaking news. Mask mandates were still far off, and our company was ahead of the game in terms of "quarantining" employees. Based on the email my coworker sent, I assumed we would be back to the daily grind in two to three weeks, but only time would tell.

Working from home was greatly beneficial during this time. I could be with my mom while she recovered, although she is stubborn and was bound and determined to get back to her routine on her own. There are many times I wished I possessed this woman's resilience and determination. After a day or two she was getting on just fine, managing her pain as she could, but taking up her daily routine, so I was kind of worthless in that respect. It just made me feel better knowing I could be available to her.

I can't even lie, though. Being with my mom with a huge bonus but work from home was always my jam. My productivity increases and working late doesn't bother me the way it does when we are in the office. Having easy access to snacks (yes, snacking is an all-day affair for me) and the ability to cook breakfast, lunch and dinner delights me. Tack on wearing yoga pants or pajamas to work, spending 24 hours a day with kitty and never wearing makeup … forget about it! Oh yeah and sleeping in until 7:30 or 8:00, still being able to get in my workout and signing on by 9:00, life is good.

After a few weeks, it got old. Just when I thought I'd be heading back to my trusty "cube", North Carolina imposed a stay-at-home order for a few more weeks. I guess my company was a trendsetter.

The fact that they put the safety and wellbeing of their employees and their loved ones first is a big win in my book. I was ready to see my coworkers and socialize, but I guess a few more weeks wouldn't hurt.

Well, a few more weeks turned into seven months, almost to the day as I'm writing this. Restaurants and bars temporarily closed, some permanently because of the economic effects. Mask wearing was mandated. Limited capacity in stores was implemented and mass hysteria ensued. Most of you reading this can probably remember a time when you went to the grocery store for chicken, milk, eggs, toilet paper, Clorox wipes, paper towels, hand sanitizer or anything canned and couldn't find a single item. There was a time when I was even starting to freak out a bit. And yes, I'm still clearing my freezer of things I wouldn't normally eat but bought in my manic state.

It is disconcerting to know we had (maybe "have" when this is published) an illness running rampant in our country, in the world, that no one knew how to treat. Even with the technology and knowledge available today, finding a cure wouldn't be simple, so we were all just watching how it would unfold and hoping for the best. People were isolated, some were dying, some were acting like absolute brats, political chaos inevitably ensued. What a time to be alive. But sometimes out of darkness comes light.

EMERGING FROM DARKNESS

Before COVID had become headline news, I was still struggling, and honestly, would continue to struggle for months. Yes, I had started to drive myself to work again, but I was still uneasy to be alone on any occasion, especially when it involved driving. I don't know if this was triggered by my episode of SVT from the prior year, the more recent stint on the heart monitor or the panic attacks, but I dreaded driving anywhere alone.

Outside of my daily commutes to work, I slowly introduced other travel into my life. The first place I tried was the nail salon. How stressful can that be, right? The salon is only about 20 minutes from my parents' house, so it felt doable. I was still a nervous wreck, but it felt good to see my favorite nail techs and get a mani/pedi after being too afraid to go in public for over a month prior.

After a successful appointment at the nail salon, I'd try a trip to my massage therapist, Jess. Dad offered to drive, but I stubbornly wanted to drive myself, which my parents did encourage. If I didn't continue to push through uncomfortable moments, I would not move forward in my progress. Driving to her house from my parents took about 45 minutes, and I stayed in my head the entire drive. All I could think about was what if I had a panic attack on the way over or while she was giving me the massage. What the hell was I going to do? Ask her to stop so I could take a Xanax and then leave? Or should I just take one when I got there so I could enjoy the massage?

That wasn't a great idea either, because I couldn't keep depending on them to get me through normal everyday situations.

Naturally, when I got there my heart was racing. As I lay face down on the table, I could feel my heart thumping the entire time. I tried to secretly do some deep breathing and be present in the moment, because Jess's massages are positively hedonistic, but I couldn't shake the fear. For the first, and hopefully only time in my life, I couldn't wait for the massage to be over. I knew my body would feel like a million bucks, but my mind was starting to look like a ball of rubber bands. I had to escape. But this was still a small win. I had driven myself and lasted the 90 minutes, so that counted for something, right?

Aside from birthday lunch with the girls, the first time I really saw any of my friends was at Abby's wedding in February. I fully planned to drive myself, as I'd been practicing more regularly now, but per usual, I stewed on it far too much. The day of the wedding, I woke up with a sense of foreboding and a lovely panic attack. How could I have been looking forward to this day for so long, and now was living in my own personal hell, unwilling and unable to enjoy anything? When I'd started the medications back in January, I thought by this point I'd be feeling more stable and confident. Wrong. Little did I know it would be months until I felt somewhat self-reliant and able to venture out alone.

There was a lot of crying the day of Abby's wedding. I hated myself. I hated the predicament I was in and hated that I might be letting her down. I really did not want to miss it, but I hadn't slept the night before and was on edge. After a lot of tears, "why me's" and mom and dad talking me off a ledge, I conceded to let my dad drive me to the wedding. More tears were to follow. In fact, many times when I got in the car with dad, especially on drives to the gym in the morning, I would lose composure and let it all flow. I just wanted to be better and felt like the day would never come.

When we got to the venue, which was about an hour away, I put on my big girl pants and my happy face and pulled it together. Dad dropped me off right at the moment that some of my favorite friends were arriving. How perfect! Having a parent drop me off made me feel like a stupid, weak child, but no one made me feel that way. True friends love you in your lowest lows and highest peaks of success.

The next few hours would be just what my heart needed. I was seated at a table with Lynny, Bry, Jen and Vince, which made me extremely comfortable to be there. They all knew what was going on and were so supportive. Mikey was there as well, and he's been my rock through everything. Even the friends I hadn't seen in forever showered me in love when I explained what I had gone through in the months prior. It felt so good to be surrounded by them, to catch up on their lives and get in some serious laughs.

Human contact outside of my parents was a wonderful thing! Hugs and catching up on my friends' lives made me feel a bit like myself again. So many lovely humans that I hadn't seen in ages were invited, and it felt like a Leroy Fox family reunion. The hugs really did it for me. Skin to skin contact with another human being is essential to maintaining stable mental health. I think these small gestures are extremely underrated and hold so much value and importance, especially when they come from people who love you.

I had a wonderful time that was mostly anxiety free. I got to see my beautiful friend Abby marry the love of her life, who was also a bud of mine. Love was in the air, and I was there to soak it up. When I started to feel a little off, dad promptly picked me up, and Lynn and Mikey made sure to see me out to the car. I will say this numerous times throughout the book, but I really don't deserve these people. They rock my world.

The next baby step on my journey was an arguably big leap depending on who was being asked (hint: mom & dad). That was driving to Lynn and Bry's by myself for an afternoon at the dog bar in late February. I hadn't been out to a bar and around strangers and alcohol since December 2019, so I was slightly apprehensive, but I was ready to do something that felt normal. The drive to Lynn's wasn't too bad, and I immediately got lap snuggles from Lukey boy (best doggie ever) upon arrival. We walked to the dog bar, taking in the spring weather and fresh air. The dog bar was full of doggie drama that day, so we ended up at a new bar called Pins Mechanical.

Pins was packed to the brim with people. It was that "you could barely walk through the place to get to the bathroom" type of packed. Normally, this would get my heart racing and send me running in the opposite direction, but I was feeling alright. I still wasn't drinking alcohol, but even took a few sips of Lynn's drink and felt fine. All of this may sound like a normal weekend day to you, but for me this was an accomplishment. I had driven myself to hang out with friends in a public place, a very busy public place, nonetheless, was around a lot of alcohol without drinking and got to enjoy the company of some pretty awesome people. One small win!

My next big move would come at the end of March. When I made the promise to myself to start driving again by late January, I also set my mind to moving home in March. Mom's surgery set the plan back a few weeks, but by God, I did it.

Living at home by myself was very scary at first. I felt uneasy spending so much time alone, although I wasn't completely alone because my sweet baby boy was there. During the first couple weeks, my dad or mom would come stay the night one or two times a week until I felt comfortable again. A part of me felt really good being home because I wanted that so badly, but it would take time to adjust.

We had been on work from home for two weeks by the time I moved home, and North Carolina had implemented their Stay-At-Home order, so I had to get used to being home alone quickly. Honestly, 2020 sucked for a lot of people, but it was not the end of the world to me. Although I was recovering from my mental breakdown In March, I was nowhere near figuring out my medication situation yet. I still wasn't comfortable carrying on a social life like I used to. I also still had random panic attacks and unprompted very dark, doomsday feelings that would come on without a moment's notice. Being at home was totally fine with me.

Restaurants, bars, shopping malls, gyms were closed. It did not affect me one bit. I think part of what helped me through recovery was the fact that everything WAS shut down. I was able to work on myself, rebuild my confidence, work on my health and fitness, develop new job skills, learn to communicate more effectively, learn to have more meaningful communication with loved ones and truly evaluate my life. Being stuck at home allowed me to move at my own pace without having to plaster on a brave face each time I exited the safety of my house for the office, a social event or trip to the gym. I am almost grateful 2020 was a shit show. It gave me extra time. Time I would have otherwise never had.

With this extra time, I found ways to fit in visits with my friends in a "pandemic friendly" way. Mikey introduced me to urban hikes, which quickly became a love of mine. Basically, I'd meet him and whoever else at a destination in Charlotte and walk around town. On my first hike, we started in NoDa at my favorite coffee shop, The Hobbyist, walked into Uptown Charlotte and then back to NoDa. This walk was incredibly special, because it's when I found out my mermaid of a friend, Jen, was pregnant with our first friend group baby. When she told me, my heart swelled to 100 times its size. How exciting! I was going to get to be an honorary auntie. It's the little things that turned 2020 into more than just a year of disappointments.

Am I happy I had a mental breakdown and got on anxiety meds? Hell no. Happy my mom got diagnosed with breast cancer, had to have surgery, and endure painful radiation treatments and medications? Happy our family trip to Europe got canceled? Happy that I didn't get to see my beautiful friend Ellie from the trip from the prior year? Happy that all my plans to travel the country and visit my friends far and wide got postponed? Happy people are getting sick and dying? Hell no to ALL of that! But dammit, 2020 taught me a lot about being grateful and healing.

In a year where multitudes of people/families are losing jobs, being evicted, unable to put food on the table, unable to provide resources for their children to continue receiving education, and so many other things, how can you possibly be down on yourself when your circumstances haven't changed?! How can anyone possibly complain? My family and friends are safe, healthy, well fed and have roofs over their heads. I haven't lost my job and am able to continue without interruption from my living room couch. I have been given the gift of time; time to grow, time to heal, time to develop healthier habits and reflect on what needs to change in order to give myself my dream life. Time to come up with this insane dream of writing this book and actually execute it. For me personally, 2020 has given me far more than it has stripped away, and for that, I am so grateful.

Anyway, now that I've said all of that, did I mention that I had ADD, by the way?! Yeah, about that: So, the next major leap on my recovery journey was a trip away from Charlotte without my family. Of course, the trip was facilitated by the one and only Lynny, supporter of all things recovery and basically all things of my life in general.

Lynny's personality trait I most love, is her ability and willingness to love and accept you as you are. There has never been a point in time between the breakdown to present day (and our entire friendship before then) when she has ever considered leaving me out or not inviting me based on my condition. She never just "forgot" about me or made the assumption I wouldn't join, even when it was pretty clear I would rather jump off a cliff than leave my parent's couch. The fact that she never gave up on me, reassured me I shouldn't give up on myself. She frequently checked in to see how I was holding up and was a listening ear, more times that I'd like to admit, when I felt like giving up. She's basically perfect, duh!

On this occasion, although she knew I was still trying to figure it all out, she invited me to the mountains in Boone, NC. It was the first weekend in June 2020, and no pressure of course, which is her signature saying. If I decided to come, I'd be rooming with Abby and Mikey, so that definitely gave me confidence in my decision to oblige. I was feeling really good about my decision until I realized I had messed up my schedule and had a hair appointment that Saturday. All that really meant was that I'd have to go up Saturday afternoon instead of driving up Friday night with my friends.

The week leading up to the trip, I drove myself crazy with worry about driving 2 ½ hours alone in the car. Being away from home for an overnight trip was a big enough shove outside of my comfort zone but driving alone on top of that was too much. This really made me sad. I didn't want to miss it, but I didn't want to drive alone. The night before the trip came, and I was distraught. The thought of all my friends having fun up in the mountains without me was such a bummer. Dammit anxiety, I hate you.

The next morning, after a conversation with my dad, he offered to drive me up to the mountains if I could ride back with Abby and Mikey the next day. My friends were completely down with that plan, but I felt so bad having my dad drive all that way up there and back. My only consolation for allowing him to drive was that he had been wanting to drive his shiny red Mazda Miata convertible up to the mountains since the day he drove it off the lot. I guess there was no time like the present.

After my hair appointment, we met up at my house and set off on our 2 ½ hour journey to Boone. The weather was beautiful and breathing in the mountain air just did something for the mind, body, and soul. Lynn didn't know I had decided to come, as I kept the secret between Mikey, Abby, and myself, so I was anxious (in a good way) to arrive and give her a giant hug.

Upon arrival, I looked at the front of the house and thought, "Um, how are we all fitting in there…" but after going inside, I was blown away. This mountain house had two full floors, with a loft upstairs from the living room and kitchen on the first floor. The main level had an open kitchen layout, living room, hardwood floors, vaulted ceilings, the standard animal head on the wall, and a rustic mountain house vibe. There were also two bedrooms and two bathrooms off to the left and a door that opened to stairs that lead down to the second level. The second level also had a kitchen, living room, two bedrooms, a master bathroom and game tables. Both floors had a full wrap around porch, with a hot tub on the main level. There were stairs off of the kitchen on the first level that lead up to the loft, which contained two beds and a gorgeous master bathroom. I would be staying up there with Abby and Mikey. The place was magnificent.

Some of Lynn's social worker friends and their significant others had come on the trip, along with our friend Kiersten and her new boyfriend. Because it was later in the afternoon, everyone was drinking, they had grilled out and food was everywhere in the kitchen. They had beer pong/flip cup set up and music was blaring. The problem was the good vibes I was fully expecting to be flowing around seemed to be stilted.

It didn't take long to realize something was not right. Someone quickly told me that some major drama had gone down the night before, and they were all glad I wasn't there for it, since they wanted me to have a great first weekend away. Aye yi yi! What could possibly have happened on a weekend away in the most beautiful mountain house I've ever seen after you've been trapped in your house for months?!

New relationship drama. *sigh*

Our friend Kiersten and her boyfriend had apparently been up at all hours of the night screaming at each other, which surely made it impossible for Mikey and Abby to sleep. The story entailed Kier's new boyfriend screaming at her for being a horrible person, ruining his birthday and drinking too much and her trying to defend herself and get him to go to bed. Honestly, if I had been there, I would have gotten out of bed to scream at them myself. No one messes with my sleep without facing the consequences.

No one wanted to go into the full spiel, but that was enough for me to understand why Kier was in a weird mood and her boyfriend was hiding in their bedroom. He was being so dramatic. Apparently, he'd also made a fool of himself the previous evening and acted out in front of everyone on the trip. Remember, this was a trip Lynn organized for her friends, so he should have been grateful he was even invited, but no, he had been kind of an ass to everyone. Now he was pouting in the bedroom, while Kier was trying to hang out with her friends.

If he was that miserable being around us and was just going to sit alone being dramatic, he should just drive home instead of staying for the remainder of the trip. I didn't want the drama around me and didn't want it for my friends either. This was supposed to be a relaxing weekend for me to try my hand at being away from home, and the bullshit could walk its ass straight out the door and keep it moving.

Lynn eventually came back outside to see I was still out there with the pup and insisted Kier come and get him so I could enjoy myself. I promptly made myself a snack and a margarita and joined my friends on the patio to catch up and relax. After another 30 to 40 minutes, Kier and her boyfriend emerge, and we learned that he was going to drive back to Charlotte. Woohoo! Get that negativity out of here!

I felt bad for her, because she was really upset, but he was being a total brat. After a drink and some hugs, she was good to go. Over the next few hours, we would play beer pong, flip cup and Cards Against Humanity, which gave me way too many NSFW laughs. I had two margaritas, which was a lot for me those days and enjoyed the beautiful weather and mountain air.

At some point during the evening, I got ridiculously anxious. It came on out of nowhere like a strong, unexpected gust of wind. I spent about two hours being awkward and mentally coaching myself through it, but everyone was so supportive and did what they could to make me feel comfortable. The feeling eventually started to fade, and I was able to enjoy the rest of the evening.

Abby was exhausted, so she went up to bed early, and I joined her shortly after. I felt a bit nervous all night and didn't get much sleep. I woke up anxious the following morning, which was quite common back then, but I still felt like I had a successful overnight stay.

The ride back with Abby and Mikey was wonderful. Catching up with two beloved friends while taking in the grandeur of the Blue Ridge Mountains in early summer, drinking Starbucks and listening to some throwback tunes is what life is all about. Despite some minor obstacles, the trip was a success. I'm so glad Lynn invited me and that I decided to follow through.

The next few months would be full of small progressions and exciting events. I would start going to brunch with small groups of friends, meeting up for dinner or to exchange books with Linds, and having friend workout dates with Amber and Laura. It felt good to be somewhat back into the groove of things, spending quality time with the friends I'd missed so much, even in the midst of having to be cautious because of COVID.

Then, much more exciting events came about! Because of the age range within our group of friends, it's only natural that there would be engagements, weddings, and babies. What a year 2020 was for all of that! Jen had already clued me in to her pregnancy, but little did I know another surprise was around the corner.

My friends Bria and Drake had been dating for quite some time and Drake had a beautiful little daughter from a previous relationship whom we all adored. For her 6th birthday party over the summer, Bria and Drake invited the girls and I to come and celebrate. We are talking a unicorn and mermaid themed party, so naturally I was all in. At the party, Bria presented Chels, Kels and I with a book and told us to open it for a surprise. Inside was an ultrasound picture! She was pregnant, too! Her and Drake had been wanting to start a family, so this was incredible news. Once again, my heart was overflowing with love.

A few weeks later, we would all join up at Bria's mom's house for the gender reveal. We were all guessing it was a boy and we were right! That evening, the girls told me that Drake had planned to propose the next day at their maternity shoot, and I could've died. Bria is one of the most kind, genuine and loving creatures I have ever met, and she deserves all the universe has to offer. Knowing she was going to get to marry the man of her dreams was exhilarating. The girls had planned to have a surprise engagement party the day following the engagement, and I couldn't wait to see her face when she walked through the door. That weekend was easily one of the highlights of my summer. In a year, where the news channels were nothing but depressing or toxic with COVID and the looming presidential election, this was the type of content we all needed.

After a late summer of birthday celebrations, baby announcements, gender reveals (we have two little boys on the way, woohoo!), surprise parties and a few relaxed months at work, I was feeling a little feisty and ready to step out of my comfort zone. COVID was giving me travel fever, something I'd lost since the mental breakdown began, and I felt the need to scratch the itch. With a worldwide pandemic in full swing, traveling presented some logistical issues, but being so close to the coast gave us options. Savannah, GA had been on my travel list for a while and would be the perfect accessible road trip to take with a few best buds.

Surprise, surprise, when this idea came up, Lynn, Mikey, and Abby, and Bry were the first people that came to mind. Lynn and I had been toying with the idea of taking a long weekend road trip, and with Bry's birthday in August, it seemed like an ideal time to hit the road and celebrate with a "Coronacation." After a lot of texts to weed through a hundred Airbnb options, Lynn finally found the perfect little house that was walkable to all of downtown Savannah.

By the time planning was complete, the trip would consist of a Friday to Sunday vacation with Lynn, Bry and Mikey. I had some reservations leading up to the trip, as this would be my first trip with several nights away from home, but I wanted to go so badly. I knew with this group that I could be myself and that if I had some type of anxious episode, they would do whatever they could to make me feel comfortable.

We left around lunch time the Friday of the trip and after about an hour in the car, I felt something shift inside me. I was actually really excited and had zero anxiety. Dang, what a freeing feeling after months of being trapped inside. Inside my house and inside my head. The weekend ended up being like a complete mind, body, spirit reset. I'm quite sure we all felt that way.

The weather wasn't fantastic, so we didn't get to go to the beach as planned, which ended up being a blessing as Tybee Island looked like COVID central when we drove out there. Instead, we made a million memories trekking around beautiful downtown Savannah, admiring the architecture, and landscaping. We jokingly picked out the homes we would buy together so we could run away forever. We explored new restaurants, drank lots of craft cocktails and bubbly and caught the beautiful Savannah sunset from the rooftop at the Drayton Hotel. We walked through the gorgeous Forsyth Park and when a popcorn vendor gave me a free bag of kettle corn, that's how I knew magic was in the air (he wasn't bad looking either, just saying).

But the best memories of all were made right there in our little Airbnb, which happened to be next to the creepiest, most haunted looking home in Savannah. Eeks! Chats around the snack menagerie in the kitchen while blasting rap music or Hamilton (Lynn and Mikey *eyeroll*), bedtime snuggles, girl time getting ready in the tiniest bathroom fit for one and hang outs on the porch until midnight... what more could a girl ask for?! Oh yeah, I forgot to mention the adventure of trying to take down the 3x4 foot menace. That was the 19th century painting of a woman that stared into your soul as you tried to sleep. It was a living nightmare hanging on the wall in the room where Mikey and I stayed. And can't forget the painting of the demon boy in the downstairs powder room that look like he'd crawled out of hell to come murder your family if you didn't turn the light on when you went to the potty. Besides that, this trip was the confidence booster and refresher I needed.

On the drive home, I spent quite a bit of time reflecting on how carefree I'd felt all weekend. That was the feeling I'd missed most over the last few years. Being carefree. Such a simple statement and such a simple act but oftentimes so difficult to achieve. Anyone with anxiety can probably understand.

Life was, and sometimes still is, such a rat race, at least for me. How do I get ahead at work? Who am I competing against to prove my worth and my position? Who do I have to impress in the office and in my personal life? Am I doing enough for my friends to make them love me? Am I being a good enough daughter/sister/friend? Did I say anything to upset someone or make them think differently of me and how do I fix it? Why doesn't everyone like me? Why can't I find a boyfriend? When will I work out tomorrow? How will I stay fit? What should I be eating and drinking to reach my ideal body? What if I gain a few pounds? What if I DON'T lose a few pounds? What if I can't fall asleep again and am unproductive the next day? What if my anxiety never gets better? When will I feel content? The list goes on and on.

None of that is healthy and none of it leads to being carefree or content. How exhausting! And therapy. How will I ever make progress in therapy if I keep on with this? How do I break the habits and change the way I think and walk through life? It was and still is all a big, complicated mess. But for those three extraordinarily exceptional days, I felt just how I'd always dreamed to feel. Perfectly situated in time and space, living a life that filled my soul with love and light and sharing it with friends that could not and will not ever be replaced.

Heading into the fall, I would continue trying to push out of my comfort zone and make weekend plans with friends. Jen and Mikey were always down for a good brunch, and Linds could always be counted on for a glass of wine. Monday nights belonged to my beloved yoga teacher, Camimi and her sunset Vinyasa Yogachellas, which always added some spice to my week. The gyms would finally be allowed to open back up at lowered capacity, and I'd head back to Cyclebar for some spin classes with my girls Erin, Stephanie, and Erika. The weekdays were spent working and, of course, working on this book.

Mid-September I'd get one of the best surprises of the year, well really of my life, because I have rarely been surprised before. Gina was my college roomie and had become one of my closest friends. She flew from Chicago to come and surprise me for a weekend. She had been keeping this a secret for weeks and my parents were in on it. They did an exceptional job pulling off the surprise.

I was so happy to have her in my home, as she'd never been

before, and she got to meet little Albie. My family loves Gina, so we got to spend some time with them over dinner at their house. Then that Sunday, Gina got to meet some of my best friends, which was the best part. Gina has been in my life so long and knows so much about me, and now I felt like she got to fully see the life I now live. She definitely took me outside of my comfort zone that weekend, which I'll elaborate on later, and gave me a weekend of excitement.

Her trip was followed by a weekend with my cousin, Lauren, whom I missed more than anything. I hadn't seen her in almost two years and was dying to have some girl time. Plus, who doesn't love an excuse to take extra PTO from work? We spent the weekend with my parents celebrating her birthday, going out to eat, shopping (our favorite) and taking a trip to Daniel Stowe Botanical Gardens. The Monday before she left, we got the most heavenly pedicures at Mimosa Nails and had lunch at my favorite Southend spot, Flower Child. Having this extra time with family was so special to me and gave me back a sense of normalcy.

A month later, one of my favorite friends, Tina, would move back from LA. This was a superb excuse to get all the friends together and celebrate. Tina's best girls from LA decided to come for a week to get her settled in and share her with us for a few days before heading back to their respective towns. The weekend was full of dinners, drinks, conversation, and late nights. I even stayed out until 10:45pm one night, which I never did anymore, and had a blast dancing the night away with my fabulous friend who was back in town for good.

Day-to-day life was improving, and I was getting back into my old routine. You may be thinking, well what can this girl complain about? She had a few rough months and now, she's back to her old ways. But nothing is ever that simple, you see.

MOVING FORWARD

I have to tell ya, I thought I was finished writing the majority of the story, but the cool thing about writing about your insane life while you're living it is that you never really run out of content. Life continues to throw shit at you from the left and right, and you just have to hope you have above average hand eye coordination.

A few weeks after I "finished" writing, shit hit the fan, AGAIN. Third quarter busy season had started up for work, and I just wasn't into it, not in the slightest. Second quarter, I felt like I thrived and really enjoyed the day to day, but during our lull between peaks, I had an enormous list of projects to complete. Once we reached Q3, I felt like I never got a break. On top of that, I was given more assignments than the previous quarter and had zero taken away.

I tried to warn my boss and director beforehand that I thought it was going to be too much, but there was really no other way to reallocate the work with our current staffing situation. Fast forward three weeks, and I'm beyond overwhelmed and miserable. I had been making some forward progress with my anxiety in terms of work, but I felt like all that progress had been washed away out into the great beyond.

I felt the pressure building about three weeks in, and one lovely Friday I just cracked. I was on the phone with with our director because one of our processes was changing significantly due to revised submissions from our business partners. I, of course, being the perfectionist that I am thought "No biggie, I can figure it out." False. My sense of dread was already high knowing the amount of work I had due in the three days following, so when I opened the new submission workbook and couldn't figure out what the hell was going on, I broke down.

I have to mention that I am not an emotional person. Crying, isn't my thing. But dammit, I sobbed on the phone with our director. It was so embarrassing, but I was so overwhelmed and so anxious that I couldn't control it from happening. I think the fact that the process was already very lengthy, and coupled with the new, confusing support just pushed me over the edge. Not to mention I had to review four workbooks over the weekend and had zero clue how to go about the review, so I was already freaking out inside. What a disaster!

Friday came and went. I worked until mid-evening and finally made some headway on my task. Saturday rolled around and it was time for Jen's baby shower. I was so excited to see my friends, but anxious and sad that I'd have to leave the shower and go straight home to log on if I want to stand a chance at getting through these assignments. The shower was so fun and beautiful, but I have to turn down everyone's invites to continue to hang out because yep… work. They guilt trip me about it and try to say it can wait, but knowing how overwhelmed I already feel, there's no way I can blow the work off.

When I got home, I was in the process of making dinner when my dad stops by for a surprise visit. It's a pleasant surprise, and I'm happy to see him for a few minutes even though I'm getting set up to start working. Once I turn on my laptop and login, the sense of dread overwhelms me yet again. So many unknowns. Assignments I've never had to complete before and having no clue where to begin just sends me spiraling. Depression, anxiety, sadness, and fear consumed every ounce of my body. I break down again, except way worse this time.

I cannot stop the tears. I'm crying so hard that my t-shirt is getting wet. I'm literally trying to drag PDFs together, and I can barely see the screen because I couldn't stop sobbing. My poor dad was sitting next to me on the couch watching this all go down and just stays there for a few minutes. Eventually he moved to the floor and watches me work.

All I can think is "How is this real life?" Why on earth do we stay in jobs that push us to this point? I enjoy my job 90% of the time, but in that moment, I absolutely hated every second of it. We were also at a point in my group where this could become the norm. Being short staffed means more work. More work is fine when you don't already have a ton to begin with, but that wasn't the case. At the beginning of the quarter, I think I anticipated this would happen, but I couldn't stop it. It's like watching a car wreck. It just goes and goes and all you can do is stand by and watch. Ugh.

I had a wellness date with Amber planned for the following day. I was terrified I was going to wake up feeling insane again but didn't want to cancel. Thank God for my instincts, because keeping that date with her was everything I needed and then some. We went to take our first live class at the new West Kept Secret studio with owner Marissa. The class was everything I dreamt of and more.

I love those women so much, because they're entrepreneurial badasses and the most welcoming, sweet, and positive coaches. With the ratchet rap music and club throwbacks blaring over the speakers, Marissa's encouragement on the mic, my friends in class with me and co-owner Heidi dancing in the lobby, how could you have a bad time? You can't, even though you may be dying from cardio overload and can't breathe, but it's fine, I promise. Ha!

Amber and I finished our wellness date with some coffee and catch up, and I finally felt a semblance of hope and relaxation. Bless it! This is just proof that sometimes, you just gotta keep it movin'. Progress isn't a straight line. It ebbs and flows. That's just how it goes. I felt like I was sliding backwards down a slippery slope, but one morning date with my girl, and I felt a little recharged.

Those few hours with Amber also opened my eyes to some improvements for the future: New career paths I could seek that better fit my personality, passions, and desires for my life. I also got suggestions on how to deepen and improve my meditation practice.

Best of all, I got a new outlook for how to recognize progress in therapy. Ninety minutes with my friend equaled incredible amounts of invaluable information and bonding time. I call that a major win.

Before my date with Amber, I really felt like I had just hit a dead end when I was trying to make massive progress. I mean afterwards, I still kind of did, but my new mindset definitely helped. Maybe it's kind of like climbing a mountain with an icy slope. You take ten steps up but slide nine steps back. Yes, that's still one step towards the goal, but getting to the top takes ten times longer. That's just kind of where I am. Life improved. Yes. I cannot deny that. I was leaps and bounds ahead of where I was back in December or January, but I still wasn't my old self. The reckless, carefree, outgoing social butterfly I once was. That's the person I want back so badly. Well, maybe not the reckless part. She can stay back in 2015.

While all this outward progress was happening, especially in my social life, the internal progress was stagnant. I had made notable changes that I can't deny. I definitely started opening up more in therapy and putting in the real work that I wasn't actually doing before. I started thinking more positively and made a concerted effort to find a few things to be grateful for each and every day. Self-reflection became a major part of my days, and I felt braver than before. But there was still a lot missing. To this day, I'm still frustrated with the progress.

I still freak out about anything health related. Yes, this is actually a huge issue for me. Every time I feel a pain, or some body part feels off for one reason or another, I freak out. I usually bombard Clarisse, who is a medical professional, with a thousand questions to make sure I'm not dying, or I text my dad a disgusting amount of times to ask if he thinks something is wrong because, for example, my armpit is hurting. At my annual physical, I always assume my blood work will tell me I am dying of some chronic disease and a normal check out at the dermatologist has me convinced I have skin cancer. Like, none of this makes sense. I know that. I am, for the most part, perfectly healthy, but in my mind, that can change at the drop of a hat.

I know I shouldn't focus on these things or even fantasize about them happening. And realistically, the above mentioned happens to regular people every single day and they end up being perfectly fine. If you have ever felt this way, I can relate, so don't feel like a complete freak like I often do. Some habits just die hard. I still ask my therapist, friends, and family if they think I'll ever "get better" or "move past this" or "get back to myself." And that's ok, because inside of me somewhere, I actually believe it's possible where I never did before.

Then there's some thought processes that are still slowly evolving. I think this part is the most challenging. For example, I still always assume I am not doing enough at work. I allow my mind to run wild when I don't immediately get feedback from one of my managers. Or, if I ping one of them something friendly and social and they never respond, I think they're mad at me or that I'm not working hard enough. Then there's the constant comparison game I'm playing in my head where I believe the managers are pitting us all against one another to see who will outperform the others. Being that I'm extremely competitive, especially in the workplace, it gets under my skin and can consume my thoughts at times.

I also need to learn to shake the sense of impending doom that lurks every single day when I logon to work and (im)patiently wait for my email inbox to load. Then, if I have received any emails from the previous evening with assignments I need to complete, I feel like a complete failure because I did not:

1. Find the issue myself.
2. Come up with the assignment on my own or
3. Stay online late enough for the person to tell me on Teams.

After I've thoroughly read through the emails and have an understanding of what needs completed, I freak out in my head about how I can get all of it done within the next hour, so as to not let down the requester of said task. I mean, clearly, some of the above listed are based in fact and reality, otherwise I wouldn't go down such a rabbit hole. Because of my experience with existing in a very toxic work environment for years, I guess those scars haven't healed.

Aside from work, I get the same raging, demonic butterflies in my stomach whenever I say something I think might have offended a friend or if someone doesn't text me back right away. I assume that the person does not want to be friends with me anymore and won't speak to me ever again. Or I spend hours combing through our previous conversations in my head trying to figure out where I could've made the turn from magical Diagon Alley to Knockturn Alley's unknown darkness. God, it's exhausting.

And let's not even talk about dating. Didn't text me until 2pm? He hates me and will never talk to me again. I was too friendly? He's scared away. I wasn't friendly enough? He's upset with me. I mean, not all of this is unrealistic because nowadays with online dating, ghosting is like the hottest trend in the streets, which most of us are guilty of at some point. But still, I need to reel it in.

Now don't get too discouraged. I'm stronger now than I was before. I'm able to at least stop myself and attempt to spin whatever is going through my mind into a positive. If I'm having a ruminating thought about something unrealistic, I'll try to distract myself or turn my attention to something more constructive. There are even occasions when I tell myself, "Fine, if you didn't do enough/aren't enough for them/upset them for no reason, that's on them, and they need to get over it." Sometimes it works, sometimes it doesn't. That's the thing. This is a never-ending journey.

We don't have the luxury of just waking up one day and it all disappears. Wouldn't that be nice? I'm medicated now and go to therapy once a week for at least a single session if not a double. We are trying multiple methods to push my progress further down the yellow brick road, but the road isn't straight. The Journey is full of obstacles, but obstacles equal growth. The problem is, you have to be hurting bad enough, perhaps even reaching a complete breaking point, to realize that the discomfort in the change and the arduous work that lies ahead is worth the reward at the end.

Some days I feel like my journey is just a straight hike right up the side of Mt. Kilimanjaro, no walking stick, a hole in my boot and only 12 ounces of water left. There are bears, avalanches, fires, snakes, barbed plants, sinkholes, you name it. Other days, it's a stroll through sunny Central Park. But the most important part of where I am now is that I'm able to tell myself that I can move forward. I started at the very bottom and am headed back towards the top.

That's the best part about having a complete and utter mental breakdown with your life falling apart at seemingly every turn is that you've been there before! You did it! You experienced your lowest lows and, tooth and nail, climbed your ass outta there and are standing tall and proud on the other side. And if you're not standing tall and proud, well I think you should be because I'm freaking proud of you, you amazing, resilient, strong, inspirational creature! And the best thing about experience is that it sticks with you. You're equipped for battle now, so if/when it ever happens again, you, my friend, have the playbook.

Although I've shared all these little tips, tricks, and golden nuggets of wisdom, I still have to remind myself of them daily. And that's ok too. We're all human. Healing, progress, growth, and transformation doesn't happen overnight. Sometimes it takes years. Think about a diamond. Once you apply a little pressure, voila! One of the most coveted, precious items in the world is born. You, my warrior, are much more precious than any diamond will ever be. So, don't give up on yourself. Keep going, and just know I'm cheering you on loud and proud over here, like that obnoxious parent at your 6th grade soccer tournament.

My story isn't over, and neither is yours, but hopefully this all helped you feel a little less like an outsider and more like you belong to some super exclusive club for people with extra special personalities and a lot more compassion and empathy than most others possess.

If I haven't bored you to death yet, and you want a few more stories, discussion points and some tactics that have worked for me, keep on reading for Part 2.

THERAPY

Therapy saved my life, but not in the ways I was initially expecting. In the beginning, I had a very distorted view of what to expect. Basically, I was under the impression that if I went to therapy for a few months, all my troubles would vanish in thin air. Just like with the medication, I had no idea what I was talking about.

When I first started going to therapy, I was really just desperate. After the disaster that was trying out Zoloft, I was determined to live a med- free life (which is a whole other subject, as previously discussed). I thought that by attending my sessions every week and participating while I was there that I would be magically cured. I thought that my therapist was just going to gift me all of these incredible tools. I thought it was a one stop fix it shop for my mental health. After years of therapy, I can tell ya that ain't how it works.

You need to show up every day. Participate. Listen. Actively listen. Answer the questions asked of you and don't say "I don't know" or "Well, it's hard." I think Ashley, my lifeline of a therapist, would say these are my two most common buzz phrases. But she doesn't let me get by with the bullshit. She pushes me. She makes me think. If I say, "I don't know," she will tell me "Okay, then think about it." She will then proceed to sit and stare at me until I have an answer. Awkward silences aren't really my thing, so typically after about 30 to 60 seconds, I come up with some reasonable answer or some counter question that will inevitably annoy her.

My sessions aren't some cake walk. There's no "Get Out Of Jail

Free" card with her. She pushes me outside of my comfort zone, but somehow makes me feel comfortable enough to share the things that bring me intense guilt and shame, some of which I've never spoken aloud to another human before. This is entirely because we have spent years developing a safe space and building a deeply trusting relationship. I hope you're starting to understand that time and patience are integral pieces of success in therapy.

You also have to remember, your therapist is not there to do the work for you, and they're not going to do the work for you. They're just there to guide you, to offer you skills, knowledge, and resources that you can either choose to take or leave when you walk out the door 50 minutes later. Just like you and me, she is professionally trained to do a job. That job is to facilitate healing not to actually do the healing. That part is your job.

That brings me to my next point: One of the most fundamental parts of therapy is finding a good therapist. What does that mean? Well, that's different for every single human being. I mean there are basics, like do they have the right education, credentials, and a decent reputation? That's obviously important to know, but beyond that, it's up to you, because finding someone is not a one-size-fits-all type scenario.

I think the first step is identifying exactly what you're going to therapy to iron out. Many therapists practice a specialty, so knowing this will help narrow down the pool a bit. Do you have anxiety, OCD, PTSD, an eating disorder, marital issues, sexual issues, identity issues, etc. The next thing is deciding if you want a male or female or if you prefer someone from the same ethnic background as yourself. What is your price range? Do you have insurance, and will you be using it? Figuring out these surface level details can give you a good base to start your research.

I'd suggest asking around and reading reviews online if you aren't confident in navigating the waters alone. If you choose to do so, proceed with caution. Therapy and therapists aren't one size fits all, that's why so many exist. What works for others may not work for you, but if you still feel uncomfortable after doing some research, a friend or family member may be able to give you a jumping point.

If you don't have insurance or don't want to meet in person, tons of options exist now for virtual therapy sessions, text therapy, phone call therapy, teletherapy, etc. If you prefer to meet virtually, some more popular options include TalkSpace, Betterhelp, Pride Counseling, Teen Counseling, ReGain and Faithful Counseling. Many of these involve weekly or monthly plans that include unlimited chat options, so that you feel connected whenever you're in need of help. The price range for these types of services tend to be more affordable than traditional therapy and work just as well. Spend some time combing through the options and educating yourself, because you want to ensure you feel the therapy is beneficial and not just another random appointment to attend weekly.

It is also important to dive into different therapy methods. Not all therapists practice the same types of therapy. There is cognitive behavioral therapy (CBT), dialectic behavior therapy, psychodynamic psychotherapy, eye movement desensitization and reprocessing (EMDR), neurofeedback and neuropsychotherapy. These are just the ones I know about. In my experience, most therapists offer some type of talk therapy, typically CBT. Ashley and I use a combination of talk therapy and EMDR to help work through my issues, while also evaluating biological factors that may come into play. Using this holistic approach, we are better able to identify what works for me and what doesn't without leaving many variables to chance.

Do some research on the types of therapy offered near you. If you see a type or two you are interested in trying, visit the websites of a few counseling locations in your area and see what they offer. Then, when you call to set up a new client appointment, you're prepared to request more information and possibly have an initial exchange with a practitioner about what to expect prior to the first visit. Many places also require intake sessions, where you and the therapist get acquainted and discuss a potential strategy to get you feeling your best.

After eliminating all variables that you can, onto the trickiest part, finding a therapist that you actually connect with, want to work with and trust. I am SO blessed and grateful that my mom called the practice I currently go to and that the woman they paired me with was absolute perfection. It took me years to fully open up to her, but if it was someone else, I likely never would have fully exposed my true self. She just gets me. We also share some common interests and can have friendly banter during the lighter sessions. That's when you know the magic has happened.

Now, don't get me wrong. I didn't walk out of my first session being like, "Oh my gosh, yes, she is a miracle worker! I must have her!" That's not factual, so I don't want you to get the wrong idea. Your first session is just like going on a date. You go, you talk, you both feel each other out, you discuss the surface level important things and see if you get a good vibe. Then if you believe it is a good fit, you go again and again.

Within the first few sessions, you should be able to gauge if it's a good match or not. At one point, I toyed with the idea of getting a therapist that was covered under my insurance. I set up an appointment, met with the woman and actually really liked her. I felt she asked the right questions and was hitting the nails on the head. Then, I went back for the second session. I felt like it was a complete waste of time. The discussion and questions hadn't changed from the first session and she just kept repeating back to me everything I was saying. It wasn't productive and the connection wasn't there. I didn't think I'd ever feel I could open up to her, even though she was very sweet, and felt her training may not be as comprehensive as Ashley's.

Keep in mind, therapy is a two-way relationship, just like with dating. When you start to meet with someone new, they might actually be the one to identify that the fit isn't quite right. Once you've made it through an intake session or two, they may decide that someone else in their practice would be a better fit for your needs. You may go in for generalized anxiety, but through your intake session, the therapist realizes that the stem of your issues is a past eating disorder and the damage it caused to your body image and self-confidence. In this instance, they may recommend switching you to another colleague. It's a two-way street, so keep your mind open.

Once you've found your match, you want to make sure that they're doing what they can to stay advanced in their field, as it will ultimately benefit you. Ashley is constantly seeking new certifications and attending training on the latest and greatest in counseling and therapy. The practice prides itself on staying advanced and likes to focus on a holistic approach to healing as opposed to just talk therapy and healing the mind. I know that if I couldn't see her for a defined period, someone else could take over for a few sessions and I'd be ok. This happened when I first went back to therapy, and while the therapist wasn't a perfect fit, she still upheld the standard of the practice and got me back into treatment while I awaited Ashley's return. These are the types of things you should be on the lookout for.

After you've found your match, it's time to begin the work. My best advice is to come prepared. Know what you want to discuss and have an idea of what you want to get out of the session. Over time I have learned that if I don't know where I want the session to take us, I don't get as much out of it. Sometimes Ashley will suggest the direction we will go by assigning homework the prior week or starting the session off with her plan, but ultimately, it's up to you. This is part of doing the work.

Therapists aren't mind readers. You're presenting your issues to them and then they will guide you through a healing process, while you do the work. As of late, I find myself taking notes on my phone or on paper when troubling thoughts arise, then I present them in my sessions. Sometimes when a certain memory or thought is really bothering me, I will text Ashley to tell her I would like to discuss the issue in our next session, so that we are both prepared ahead of time.

You won't have to do this every time, because often, you will work on one topic for several weeks. But I've also learned that sometimes seemingly unrelated issues are all linked together by similar themes, so bring forth what comes to mind. I'm discovering all this as Ashley and I dig deeper into the bizarre and scary inner workings of my mind.

For example, I brought up a scenario where I got overly anxious because I thought someone at work was trying to sabotage me. I was giving her this example as proof that I wasn't making the improvement I desired with my anxiety. I thought to myself that if I were making progress, I'd be able to talk myself off this stupid ledge. Then Ashley flips everything I believe on its head and tells me that perhaps, it's not my GAD causing the issue but how I view myself as a person instead. She said that if I was confident in myself, loved myself and was authentically myself 100% of the time, that I wouldn't feel so anxious in these scenarios.

Let me tell you something, I do NOT like it when she's right and normally I will not admit to her being right. In this instance though, I felt like she might be onto something. And to be honest, it gave me a sense of relief to know that maybe we finally found a root cause of my issue and that with time, I could work on that root cause and climb up out of my anxiety hole. She's been bringing me back to this self-image point time and time again, but like I said before...time and patience. I didn't see it in the same light she did until that session.

Aside from being prepared for sessions, I also suggest making an effort to try any techniques offered by your therapist outside of the sessions. Without working on the techniques provided, they will never provide any relief or change. I cannot tell you that amount of times she has given me a tool that I've tried for a few days, but it doesn't work. Then I'm feeling all hopeless and irritated that it didn't work for me but has worked for several other people. Those things didn't work because I gave up, not because the tool didn't work. Remember, you're not some miracle person who is so abundantly different from the rest of humankind that nothing will work for you. You're special, but just not in this scenario. Yes, this is another lesson I learned.

When you feel like a caged animal and will do anything to get out, you want a quick fix. That's how I was for the first two years of therapy. Ashley offered techniques such deep breathing, box breathing, tapping, counting, journaling, meditation, mind dumping, the GLAD technique and more. Some of these worked quite well, and I should've stuck with them.

Tapping in particular worked great for me. Basically, you take a scenario you are worrying about and come up with four or five positive truths about the outcome. Then you tap on your fingertips or leg while you say the statement. It is a grounding technique. For example, I used this when I was taking the CPA exam. I would come up with statements like "I am smart." "I can pass this test." or "This test doesn't define me." Then you tap either once per syllable or once per word, it is really your preference. You don't want the statements to become too long or complicated, because then you're more concerned with the process than the actual grounding technique.

For more everyday use, I would say things like "I am strong and resilient." "I can survive anything." "I am safe and loved." Then on rough days, I would tap on my leg in the car or in my seat at the office. It's a good way to hammer a positive affirmation in your mind while performing a grounding technique. Two birds, one stone. You get the idea.

I also used the GLAD technique for a prolonged period of time until I came up with my own system of gratitude journaling that works best for me. GLAD stands for Gratitude, Learning, Accomplishment and Delight. Each day you will write something you're grateful for, something you learned, something you accomplished and something that delighted you. It can really be anything. Here's an example:

G - I'm grateful for a visit from my dad during work today.
L - I learned how to French braid my hair.
A - I accomplished all the document linking that needed updating for our Q4 filing.
D - The breakfast tacos I made this morning were delightful.

You can find a multitude of information on this technique on the interwebs, but this is a little preview. I suggest giving it a try for a few weeks and then going back and reading what you wrote. It can be kind of fun to see what happened over time that you've already forgotten about. Plus, you can see how much you've learned or accomplished, which is always a great feeling.

As you can see, you may need to try a few techniques until you find one that works for you, but once you find one, you're good to go. You don't need a toolbox with a hundred tools. You need to have two or three reliable and trusty tools that can be used time and time again.

Don't do what I did and overwhelm yourself by trying five or six new things at once. Take one at a time, try them for two to three weeks, and if you're still not seeing any relief, then try a new one. I will recommend, however, that you find a foundational deep breathing technique to work on and develop as one of your tools. This works for the majority of people and can be useful in a number of scenarios.

Now that you have your therapist, you have your tools and you're doing the work, you will start to discover so much about yourself that you may have never known. Therapy taught me so much about my strength and resilience. It also taught me how to be more kind, compassionate and loving to myself and others. It has helped me shape the way I think and the way I evaluate different life scenarios. And most importantly, it's teaching me that I'm not alone. Nothing is wrong with me. I'm just a regular gal out here trying to better myself.

That's one point I want to hammer home. One common misconception people might have about therapy is that something has to be "wrong with you" for you to need therapy. I felt this way a lot in the beginning because I didn't know anyone else that had a therapist. The truth of the matter is that therapy is for everyone. It does not matter how well-adjusted you are, or how easy your life is, or how happy you are. Everyone has something that they can work on.

I am actually starting to believe that most of us actually do live with a clinical mental health issue but most of the time it goes unrecognized. Maybe it's because mental health issues are so stigmatized, or people are afraid of what they may find out about themselves. To this day even my most well-adjusted friends will admit to me that they feel like they need to talk to a therapist about at least one or two matters in their life. Some of them even think they suffer a mental health condition that they've never had diagnosed and have hidden from the world. But you don't have to have a diagnosed mental health condition to start trying to resolve issues from your past or work through something difficult in your present or even talk about your fears for the future.

Therapy is about overall wellness. Wellness is both mind and body and taking that time to explore your mind and work on self-improvement is imperative to total health. This brings me to another point. Don't let anyone make you feel guilty about prioritizing therapy over other activities, even your job.

I always felt guilty, and occasionally still do, when I must leave work to go to therapy. For the longest time, I was the only person in my group at either of my jobs that went to therapy. This was just another isolating fact, that initially made me feel alone and weird. But regardless, it always was difficult for me to ask my manager if I was allowed to leave for the day or to tell them that I had to go to therapy that day at a certain time.

I always felt guilty leaving when other people had to stay and work, and I was just going to talk about my problems. I felt like I couldn't make it a priority over staying late to work on a project. When I was at my first accounting job, these feelings would occasionally lead to me canceling a session last minute. I felt easier to just stay at work and eat the cost of the session than attempt to leave for my session. It also didn't help that I had to drive 30 minutes to get there from the office and had scowling coworkers when I had to leave.

When I started my new role, the office was much closer to the practice, but that didn't make me feel any less guilty about leaving, especially during busy season. At that point I was accustomed to feeling guilty about leaving work any time before six or so and therapists don't normally practice late into the night, so you have to try to get your sessions in at a decent hour. After a few months at my new job, the guilt started to diminish as I realized that my mental health was far more important than my job. (I mean, I love my job and it's obviously very important to me, but … priorities.) Now I just politely ask during busier peaks if it's alright to leave, move my sessions on days that I know will be too hectic and do double sessions when possible to make up for any lost time.

I no longer feel weird, embarrassed, or guilty about going. I'm open when talking about therapy and happy to recommend it to others. Ashley has become an indispensable part of my human solar system. She's the most unbiased, supportive, encouraging light that helps lead me on my way. She knows how to challenge me and push me towards being my best. She never lets me quit and calls me on my bullshit. I honestly don't know what I'd do without her. If you just give therapy a try, I know you can find your very own Ashley, too. Even though it's hard work, there are often tears involved and you have to purposefully get uncomfortable, the payoff is worth the agony. You will never regret the time you took to mold you into a better you!

Carrie Thompson

BODY IMAGE ISSUES:
WHAT A BEAST!

For the majority of my life, I have struggled with body image issues. I think many of us have struggled at some point or another with being comfortable in our own skin and loving our bodies, men and women alike. There is constant pressure to keep up with the times and the standards projected onto us by society. Whose bodies are being put up on society's pedestal and admired? What are the latest trends in fitness and dieting? How do we think we are supposed to look based on our peers? What are our health and fitness goals? And mostly importantly, how the hell do we keep up with it all? For me, it's been a long, long journey to feeling confident, finding true health, and learning to appreciate my body more for what it can do than how it looks.

Since I was young, I struggled with my weight. I was always the fat kid. From my earliest days in elementary school, I can remember being bullied for being fat. I have a horrendous long-term memory, but I will never forget the time one of my neighbors compared my size to the Titanic crashing into the iceberg.

Even when I was little, I noticed that my peers were much more petite than me, much cuter, smaller, and athletic. I was the fat girl that, luckily, some people wanted to befriend. Once my friends and I were reaching 5th and 6th grade, they were getting attention from boys, getting boyfriends and dressing in the coolest styles. No boys were ever interested in me because I was the fat girl with the big bushy eyebrows, fat round face and short haircut that crested around my chin making my face look even chubbier.

As for the cute clothes, my size often presented an issue when it came to finding the more popular styles. When I was in 5th grade, I was already a size 11 in junior's jeans where my friends were a 5 or 7. Dang, do you guys remember the store 5-7-9? I know, let's make a store advertising to teenagers that the respectable sizes to wear are 5, 7 or 9, and if you're bigger (or smaller) than that, you'll have to shop elsewhere. I mean this was the 90's and early 2000's, so body image issues weren't quite a hot topic yet, but what a way to set the future generations up for toxic thinking and comparison games.

But like I said, mom and I often had trouble finding the latest styles in my size, and if we did find my size, I had to assess whether the clothes were actually flattering or not. I will never forget the time that my friend's moms had all gone to Gabe's while we were at a school event and found the coveted JNCO jean shorts we had all been drooling over. They were extremely overpriced, but if you were a 90's kid, you probably fell into this fad or at least know what I'm referencing. If you don't know what Gabe's is, picture a giant, sterile looking store with bright fluorescent lights and grey and white tiled floor with row after row of hanging racks filled with deeply discounted clothing. They also sold shoes, housewares, accessories, etc. It was basically like a B grade version of TJ Maxx or Home Goods.

Anyway, so my friends told me their moms had found them the perfect JNCO jean shorts to rock for summer. They had about a three-inch inseam that hung around your hips and hit way below your belly button. Think Christina Aguilera style when she was just becoming popular. After getting this groundbreaking news, I promptly sent my mom to hunt for the shorts. She got to Gabe's, located the shorts, but the only ones in my large size were longer and hit a little above the knee. I still wanted them, of course, because hello, JNCO's, but what a disappointment. My oversized waist had struck again.

And let's take a moment to reflect on the female icons of the 90's. First up is Britney Spears and Christina Aguilera. So many of us girls all but worshiped them. Boys got googly eyes over them and girls envied their looks and talent. They danced around in their music videos in their skimpy outfits displaying their flat stomachs and thigh gaps. Then there were the Spice Girls; Beautiful, thin, and British. I always wanted to be Posh Spice, the thinnest and most elegant of them all. Always displaying her slender frame in a barely-there form fitting dress. We also had TLC, Destiny's Child, Cher, Dionne from Clueless and who could forget the girl next door, Kelly Kapowski, from Saved by the Bell? All different, but all thin, gorgeous, and iconic in their own perfect way. These were the images I looked up to and ones I so desperately wanted to emulate. But I couldn't. I would never be that thin, that beautiful, that desired.

Back then, there was no "all bodies are beautiful" mindset. Thin was in. That was it. No one was accepting of larger bodies. There was no body positivity or self-acceptance if you weren't the ideal size, weight or look. Being fat was considered plain wrong and something that needed to be fixed. As a matter of fact, curvy wasn't as accepted either. Some bodies are just made differently. Bigger butts, bigger legs, bigger boobs. But if you didn't have a thigh gap...yikes! Diet culture was on the rise and thriving. SlimFast, Weight Watchers, Atkins Diet, Zone Diet, South Beach Diet, diet pills, anything low-fat, no-carb, no sugar and lots of processed "meal replacement" beverages. If you grew up in the 90's and 2000's, guaranteed you or someone you know tried at least one of these diets. We were being set up for failure.

My size was very isolating, at least on the inside, and I wasn't necessarily pretty either, especially compared to my peers. I spent a lot of time dreaming of looking like those iconic celebrities or even one of my classmates. You know, the popular pretty girls. The ones who became cheerleaders, got picked for homecoming, got asked to the dances and on dates in those really fun Instagrammable ways before cell phones could even take pictures. Why did I have to be the ugly duckling? It sucked, and it thoroughly and totally sucked and would affect me in ways I couldn't even have imagined, leaving lasting scars that I'm still trying to heal.

When we entered middle school, the difference in how I looked compared to peers became even more apparent as all of the elementary schools in my district combined into one middle school and I saw the girls from the other schools. Of course, I wasn't the only bigger girl, but I felt like we were the minority. Luckily, I had amazing friends and still had so much fun but longed to be the attractive girl that everyone wanted.

I would frequently fantasize about the day that I would actually have my first boyfriend or fall in love. I prayed every single night that he would come into my life. Year after year I prayed and prayed, but nothing ever really changed. This praying would continue for decades and is still a part of my daily routine.

Once we left middle school and went to the high school, I spent one final year as a fat girl. By this time, I was damaged. My mental health had already been terribly affected by the bullying and comparison games that I played every day. I still had my crowd of friends that I fit into, but the ways I would go about getting attention weren't always the most positive.

I was very loud and obnoxious. I would always try to be funny or be "one of the boys." Since they wanted to date my friends and not me, I guess I could try to fit in with them. Most of the time it worked, so while I wanted to be thin, beautiful, feminine, and popular, I was loud, boisterous, obnoxious, and sassy. Attention, but not the kind I longed for.

Freshman year, I was a band geek, which was extremely fun, and I joined the swim team. These were my people, so at least I found where I fit in. My three best friends from when I was five years old, Sammi, Dianna and Donna, did all the same activities, so it was great having them around. And with marching band practice starting in the summer, I got to make some really amazing high school friends before school even began that fall. That year was cool and all, but the real issues surfaced that summer.

I'm not sure what really drove me to this point, but I slowly cracked. As a teenager, it never occurred to me what I was actually doing until years later, but looking back, I was in a very bad place. That summer, I started working out. A lot. I went to the local YMCA every day and worked out for hours. I would run on the track or treadmill or get on the Stairmaster. I would bring books to read or have my cd player. That definitely dates me. Do any of you remember having to walk or run with a full-blown cd player in your hand? Kids have it so good these days. No gigantic circular plastic device with headphone cords getting twisted all over the place and foam ear pad coverings you had to squeeze out after every workout because they got sweaty. Oh, the memories.

As the months passed, I became obsessed with working out and have never stopped since. On top of the working out, I all but stopped eating. Every day, I would wake up, do whatever teenagers do in and morning and then lounge around watching TV. My "meal" consisted of one SlimFast bar. I think the cinnamon raisin and chocolate chip were my favorites. I would eat the bar, but so slowly that it would last an hour. I would break it up into dime sized pieces, roll them into balls and eat them. This would be my only meal until dinner that evening. Dinner, I can't really remember, but at the time it was probably a small portion of whatever my mom made. If I got hungry in between, I would eat carrot sticks with peanut butter. I didn't realize at the time, but I was becoming anorexic.

That summer, I went from weighing 170lbs to 135lbs. I was really thin. Three months, 35lbs gone. My hip bones stuck out so far, and I loved it. I was wearing tighter tanks to the gym and shorts low slung on my hips so that my hip bones were showing. I had made some girlfriends at the gym, Amy and Megan, who I came to discover suffered the same way I did. I would run with them, workout with them, take diet pills with them, you name it. They weren't enabling me, but they weren't stopping me either. I felt a special connection with them because we were all suffering with the same affliction: Very serious body dysmorphia. That was another word I didn't learn until years later.

When I went back to school in the fall, I think people were a little shocked. What happened to the chubby girl that used to wear the Billabong t-shirts and parachute pants? Now she was rocking Hollister jean skirts and sheer graphic tees layered over a spaghetti strapped tank. Don't worry. We all got checked every morning to make sure our spaghetti straps weren't showing and that our skirts passed the fingertips rule. You remember, the rule where your skirt or shorts had to stop below your fingertips? Otherwise, you got sent to the principal's office and your parents called so they could bring you new clothes.

Anyway, the chubby girl that was bullied was still there inside my head. She never left, and she's honestly still there. Past versions of yourself never truly leave. Sophomore year, I still thought I was fat. 135lbs was not thin enough. I needed to break into the 120's, then maybe I'd be happy. My eating habits that year didn't change much. I had a SlimFast bar at breakfast and Diet Coke for lunch. Occasionally before swim practice I'd share a little packet of donuts from the vending machine with my friend Sammi. After practice I'd eat a bagel and trail mix or something similar.

Bagels were my favorite dinner. Panera was a hot commodity back then, and when we'd go shopping on the weekend, we'd bring some back from Pittsburgh because our little town didn't have a location yet. I honestly think the bagels kept me functioning. Our bodies seem to handle just about anything during that age.

Every day after swim team practice, I'd come home and all but collapse on the couch. After working out and a two-hour swim practice, my body was ready to shut down. I'd eat my bagel dinner, sometimes with fat free ice cream and trail mix on top. After that, I would lay down on the loveseat and close my eyes. They never said anything, but I'm sure my parents were becoming concerned. I kept on like this for over two years, but eventually I'd start eating normal again.

Sophomore year, I had my first boyfriend. I had expanded my friend group and started hanging out with people outside of my close circle from elementary school. Through my new friends, I met Mike. He was a tall, handsome, good ol' country boy. I probably should've tried to date him for the long run, but that didn't work out when his ex-girlfriend pulled my hair at a dance and tried to fight me because of him. What a mess. When I backed away, he drove an hour to get me my beloved bagels, but I refused to see him. Who knows what I was thinking back then?

Over the next few years, my obsession with food and working out would worsen. I was obsessed with calories, when I was going to eat, what I was going to eat, how much I was going to eat and how I was going to keep losing weight. Of course, once your body gets so thin, it goes into starvation mode and holds onto every last ounce of you that exists. That's where I was by junior year. No matter how many hours I worked out and what I ate, I couldn't get any smaller. I didn't get fat again, but I had gained weight and hated it.

I also had stretch marks. Lots of stretch marks. Some because of genetics, some because of how overweight I was before and some because of how quickly I lost the weight. If there was one thing I hated more than being fat, it was having stretch marks. I had never seen other girls with so many stretch marks on their legs, tummy, and sides. I was appalled when I looked at myself. Years later, I would learn that most women (and some men, too) have stretch marks. They're just another part of your body to embrace. Maybe those marks are badges of honor from birthing a beautiful child or from a hard-fought battle with weight loss. Or maybe they're just marks left there to remind you we are all human and should love the skin we are in, because it doesn't define who we are internally.

Because of my irritation with how I looked and my inability to get smaller, I started to acquire a diet pill problem. My friend Amy worked at GNC, so I would go see her at work and she'd show me the latest ones. I'd always save up my money for these big purchases and would take them every day. I didn't realize at the time how terrible they are for you and that they did absolutely nothing to help you lose weight. Unless, of course, you could find the ones with ephedrine in them before it became illegal, but that's neither here nor there.

I was on a dangerous downward spiral with my body image and my mental and physical health. I had a few more boyfriends over the next couple years, which made me believe that being thin made it possible for someone to actually want me. Forget about my personality. At least I looked ok. None of these were boys from my high school, but once our friend groups started commingling with kids from other schools, I was able to meet them. The relationships never lasted long, and I never demanded the proper courting I deserved. This unhealthy habit would follow me well into the future.

Because of my low self-esteem, I started hanging out with an unsavory crowd. At the time, I told myself that I was friends with everyone and anyone, because I was brought up not to judge people. Looking back, I question the decisions I made and live with a lot of shame and regret for the situations I got myself into. All of this started because my friends were becoming more beautiful and more popular, and I was just falling more behind. I didn't feel like I fit in at all anymore and I craved a sense of belonging. Unfortunately, the sense of rejection I felt led to a terrible senior year and a loss of lasting memories I could've made with my lifelong friends who had loved and accepted me for me my entire life.

After graduation, the real countdown until college began. I had gotten accepted to Ohio State University in the fall, accepted the offer in January and was ready to start my new life with a clean slate. I couldn't wait to get away from my small, close minded hometown and start a new life. The future was so bright. I even thought that maybe this would be my opportunity to meet a man, fall in love and live happily ever after. I'm sure you've noticed a pattern by now, but I'm frequently wrong and this college dream life I created was no different.

This chapter is really about body image, so I won't go into all the other freshman year college drama, the bad roommates, the bullying, the having to move dorms, or the feeling so homesick I wanted to move home stuff. The highlight of my freshman year was being put in Morrill Tower for my freshman year dorm, because it was right next to the freshly built, state of the art athletic facility, the Ohio State Recreation and Physical Activity Center (the RPAC).

The RPAC was the most beautiful sight I had ever seen. When I had gone on my initial campus tour earlier in the year, it was still being built and we could not get a tour, so stepping inside the facility for the first time was an other-worldly experience. This place was athletic facility heaven. Floor upon floor of brand new, state of the art fitness equipment.

If you entered from the bottom level and walked up the stairs, you were met with the juice bar and cafe. On the floor above you had tons of cardio equipment, workout areas, meeting rooms, offices, basketball courts, you name it. Then down on the main level there were rows upon rows of cardio equipment, the pool, basketball courts, racquetball, locker rooms and a gigantic weight room with every weight, band, machine, mat, and ab equipment that existed. This was my favorite place on campus by far.

Having this incredible facility less than a five-minute walk from the doors of my dorm building was a double-edged sword. It made me so happy but also fed into my workout obsession. I would spend two or more hours a day there, mainly on my favorite cardio equipment, the ARC trainer. It is kind of a cross between a step machine and an elliptical, and I'd never seen one until I'd come to Ohio State. I spent countless hours on that thing. I studied for exams by propping my notes up on the book holder. I watched football games and trashy TV shows. Most importantly, I met my best friend, Clarisse.

After meeting up a few times in the gym, we were inseparable, at least from a workout perspective. It was a fast and easy friendship, and we were both gym obsessed crazies. There was a 30-minute limit per piece of cardio equipment, and people would check your time and wait impatiently to get on after you. We combatted this by covering our monitors with a gym towel or sweatshirt and restarting the machine every 30 minutes, so no one ever really knew how long we had been on there. Sometimes we would stay on for two hours at a time together. It was bad.

Because I had started drinking and eating fast food, keeping weight off and attempting to lose even more was definitely difficult. I obsessed about trying to eat 1,200 calories or less and was obviously overtraining in the gym. This was a deadly combination, as my body was back in starvation mode, feeding off the excessive amounts of alcohol and trying to recover from my two to three hours a day in the gym. Nothing about this was healthy.

On top of my physical health, my mental health was suffering too. I was so homesick and was having issues with my dorm mates. Luckily, after the Christmas break, I moved to a different floor and life improved. I had found my people and started going out and partying more. I was at a Big 10 school with one of the best football programs in the country and 50,000 other young adults who were ready to be independent of their parents. Of course, things got a little wild, but for me, this environment exacerbated my existing body image issues and attention seeking behaviors.

With alcohol now involved and inhibitions lowered, the increasing desire to attract a mate or become popular, and a brand-new playground in front of me, life spun a little out of control. I was going out almost every night with my girlfriends, skipping class, drinking way too much, saying things I don't remember, doing things I barely remember and waking up with regret.

For the duration of my college tenure, I spent an exorbitant amount of money on drinking and going out. Thousands upon thousands of dollars buying drinks for me and my friends. I spent at least six nights a week at the bars or clubs with my girls being wild and trying to get guys to talk to us. I dressed far too sexy to try to attract attention and spent countless nights out grinding away with my girlfriends on the dance floor to see who would buy us a drink. I thought this was the way to a good man's heart. Get drunk, dress sexy, dance scandalously with your girlfriends, find a hot drunk guy, make out, get his phone number … you know the drill. False!

Of course, all my girlfriends in college were thin and gorgeous, and I was still my awkward attention seeking self from high school. I mean my looks had improved, but I was lacking in many areas. I wasn't great at dressing fashionably and I sucked at applying makeup. Still to this day, I am terrible in both of these realms. I'm one of those "looks girly but has no idea what they're doing" type of females.

Yeah, I was a mess. I was lost, unfocused, depressed, reckless and attention seeking. I used alcohol to make me feel better and attention seeking techniques to feel wanted and valued. Clearly this did nothing for me. I left college without a clear career path ahead, an extra 15 extra pounds thanks to all the drinking and 3am stops to the gyro truck and more shame for all the mistakes I'd made along the way.

Yet again, I wanted to start over. I randomly decided I would move to either Atlanta or Charlotte and in the summer of 2010. I made the final decision that Charlotte would be my new home. I was hopeful to quickly meet friends, find a corporate career and build the life I'd always dreamt of, including a husband and family. But life doesn't always work out in the manner you have planned in your head.

I will just sum up my first few years here like this: Nothing changed from college. Simple as that. I still worked at a bar job. I got into a friend group that did nothing but party, drink and stay up until the wee hours of the morning. I was still attention seeking. I still had body image issues and obsessive workout habits, and I was still single.

The worst part, though, was how jealous I'd become of the people in my circle. My jealousy would heighten when I was intoxicated to the point that I would take out all of my internal pain on the people that cared about me most. After five vodka Redbulls and four shots of tequila, I was evil. I would get unbelievably angry with my friends if something did not go my way. And if I didn't get angry, I was an emotional mess. Why can't I meet someone who will love me? Why is this so hard? Why am I so undesirable? What is wrong with me?

Man, that shit was hard and sucked so much. I spent so many mornings trying to piece together the garbage I'd said to my friends the night before and then trying to make up for it so that I didn't lose them. I think the real awakening came when I went to visit Gina in LA. The first night I was out there, Gina and I went out with her roommate and a few of her new LA girlfriends. I really don't remember what happened, but all I know is that my behavior was atrocious.

I know I had to have offended her girlfriends and made them wonder why on earth she'd even associate with me. The next morning, I woke up in shambles. Gina was at work, and I called my dad to tell him I needed to fly home immediately. I knew I had majorly fucked up. Because of my idiotic behavior, I was losing one of the best friends that I had made in life. I got a last-minute flight back to Charlotte and sat in LAX for 13 hours waiting to board because I couldn't stand to see her when she got home from work. What kind of person had I become?

This may all seem unrelated, but do you see how my terrible self-esteem and body image issues from when I was so young had spiraled out of control and started affecting every facet of my life? That's why I want to share all of this with you. I know I'm not alone. I know there are other people out there deeply hurting with similar experiences. Just know that on the other side of the dark, dank forest, there is hope and sunshine and all that other hippy stuff I love now.

From the moment I had ruined my friendship with Gina, I knew I had some serious work to do internally. Thank God, years later she would forgive me and give me a chance to redeem myself. I didn't wake up the next day a changed woman or flip some switch that turned my behavior around. It took years to break these terrible habits.

I still drank too much and would mouth off to friends for no good reason other than I was feeling "threatened" by them and full of jealousy or not getting my way. God forbid I have interest in some guy, and he hit on my friend. I would take it out on her in some stupid made-up argument I'd invent later on in the night. None of it made sense. I was a walking disaster, especially when I was drinking. Over time, I got my temper under control, and I'm proud of myself for that. However, the jealousy, body image issues and low self-esteem stuck around. Eh, I mean, they still kind of linger to this day, but I am on a continual path of self-improvement and all that.

Changing the way you feel about yourself takes a lot of work. Becoming healthy takes a lot of work. If you are set up to believe a set of beauty standards from a young age, it becomes programmed in your head. It's not exactly easy to break free of those chains. I mean, think about it, I really started noticing these things when I was around five years old, and I didn't even know what an eating disorder, body dysmorphia or overtraining was for almost two decades. That's a long damn time to have the same thoughts revolving over and over in your head.

No one talked about these things when I was young. No one. I knew I chose not to eat but didn't know there was a name or disorder associated with it. Because I was a bigger girl, I thought working out was the thing to do. No one told me that two or three hours a day was destroying my lean muscle mass and causing me to hang onto body fat. No one taught me that bigger bodies were beautiful. Not for years and years.

When I was in college, some of my friends wore their eating disorders like a golden badge of pride. It was ok to pick at your food or skip meals. I'm sure for most of college, I didn't even eat breakfast. For some girls, that's how they stayed thin all of college even after going on drinking binges for days at a time. I mean, hello freshman 15! No one spoke about how disordered eating was dangerous and could damage your body and metabolism long term. I was back to eating more towards the end of high school and all through college, but the mental damage had been done.

The overtraining was a much harder habit to break. Working out was an addiction. I honestly don't even know if I liked it, but I knew I had to do it, and I thought I had to do it for hours a day. Sometimes multiple times a day. Then when fitness trackers came along, the habit became even more toxic. Once I got one of those babies, I was constantly focused on how many steps I'd taken or how many calories I'd burned in relation to what I ate that day.

I'm currently 33 about to be 34. From the time I was 13 until about the time I was 31 or 32, I worked out obsessively. I never took days off. I never gave myself a break or a light workout. That just would not do. It took me nearly twenty years to figure out that less was more. Honestly, one of the biggest influences that changed the way I viewed fitness was Sydney Cummings. The community that she has built as a result of her amazing YouTube channel helped me to get over the hump of my workout addiction.

Slowly I started training using only her videos or going to spin classes. My workouts went from two hours a day, sometimes longer with two workouts in a day, down to an hour or less. And dang it, I was actually seeing results! I had real muscles now, not a bunch of deflated body parts that were sick and tired of all the abuse they had endured. I began to appreciate strength training and HIIT training instead of just hitting the treadmill or Stairmaster for hours on end.

And with that, I got so much time back. Oh, and also saved a ton of money since Sydney strives to make fitness accessible to everyone. Her workouts are Free99. Follow her on YouTube!

I stuck with Sydney's plan and slowly started adding in more varied workouts like my spin classes and workouts at various other boutique studios around Charlotte. Meeting new women in the fitness community, my eyes were opened up to all the options out there. Some of my favorite additions have been my West Kept Secret classes, yoga classes, especially sunset yoga with Camimi, and of course, my Peloton. Along with the new classes I was exposed to, I also gained some incredible inspiration and role models.

While I loved all my gym friends and workout buddies I'd acquired over the years, we all shared some unhealthy habits. With the new path I was on and the new role models in my life, I was finally starting to see what true health and wellness meant. It's about appreciating what your body can do, NOT what your body looks like. We are so much more than aesthetics. One of my favorite humans/cycle instructors/body-positivity role models, Meagen, used to preach to us that we were all athletes. We should all be proud of ourselves for getting out there and trying no matter what our ability level was, how far we were into our fitness journey or what we looked like. We should be proud of just showing up! Truer words have never been spoken.

I was finally starting to figure it out. On top of shaving down the time of my workouts, my incredible health coach friend Alexandra convinced me to start taking rest days. That was a hard one. You mean completely not workout at all? I will die. I will gain 20lbs. I can't possibly have a day off. Nope. It's actually fine, and I'm still alive. Not working out doesn't always mean sitting around like a bump on a log, which actually is totally fine if you do, but I just go on walks. Because I sit at a computer all day, I need to get in movement so walks it is, and I love every second of it.

Days off were emphasized even further when I hired my badass nutrition coach, Finley, whom I also met and followed because of Alexandra. I knew I finally had my workouts under control, but something was still missing in the nutrition piece. When I first reached out to her, we discussed my background with disordered eating and what I was trying to achieve on this journey. Of course, my answer was "fat loss," but didn't realize that reaching that goal actually meant eating more food. After tracking for a week and reporting to Finley that I was eating around 1,600 calories a day or less, we had some work to do. When she sent me my personalized macro-based goal plan, I saw that I was going to have to eat MORE food which is known as reverse dieting. This didn't seem intuitive to me at all, but she explained that in order to safely lose weight, I'd first need to be eating an appropriate amount of calories to fuel my body.

For someone that would tack an extra hour on to their workout if they ate something fried or had a few too many drinks, this did not sit well. This nutter was telling me to eat more food and informed me that eating fried food and sugary goodness was fine (in moderation, of course). What was this alternate reality?! But, you know what? I hired her because I trusted her, so I was going to give it a shot.

The results of following her plan astounded to me. I was actually getting thinner, more toned and stronger. My body composition was shifting because I was fueling it properly. I was achieving so much more by paying attention to the distribution of carbs, fats, and proteins I was eating each day and learning to eat more intuitively. I was sleeping better, worrying less about what I ate, eating carbs, and having more energy. Before this I was literally eating chicken and veggies for every meal. When I stopped drinking caffeine back during my mental breakdown, I thought I was doomed. With this new eating plan, I had far more energy than I ever did with coffee.

More importantly, as I continued to work with her and trust her, I developed healthier habits, a greater appreciation of true health and wellness, and started to repair the body dysmorphia I'd acquired decades before. She promoted loving your body at every stage of your journey and accepting that anything worth having takes time and patience.

This whole process with Finley took much longer than I anticipated. I was in a reverse diet for over a year, but don't regret one second of it. Going into the cut, I was excited for what we could achieve, but was not excited about it like I was when we first started working together. Giving up the extra food that I had learned to love and began to depend on, had become a disappointing prospect. This was a sign that the mental health progress I was making in relation to my body image was actually sticking. Oh, and by the way, at the end of the reverse diet, I was eating over 2,500 calories a day and had only gained one pound. I hope this tells you something.

This whole journey has been excruciating. My heart is broken for the little girl that thought she was worthless because she was overweight, had stretch marks and was average looking. I want to wrap her in my arms and tell her that looks really aren't everything and that true health goes much deeper than surface level aesthetics. Every single person has so much to offer and deserves to be loved for more than what is on the outside. In fact, they should be loved based solely on what is on the inside.

Do I still obsessively plan out my workouts every week? Yeah, sometimes. But often, I am flying by the seat of my pants on what I will do to be active. Do I worry about closing all my activity rings on my Apple watch every day? Sometimes, but that's not really a concern these days. Do I obsessively weigh and track every single piece of food that enters my mouth? Nope! I plan for the day and if I have a few untracked snacks or bites of food, it's alright. I won't die. I won't gain 10lbs. I'll probably forget about it later that day or the next morning. Do I worry about what size pants I wear and how my body looks? I mean, yes, I do. I work hard and I want my body to reflect that, but it's no longer the end of the world if there's some backwards progress.

The tall, thin, surgically enhanced bodies I used to admire aren't really my ideal anymore. If this is you, more power to ya, sis! I think you should do whatever makes YOU feel beautiful, and if that's a gorgeous pair of fake tatas or some lip injections, good for you. Own that shit.

Now I look to my role models for being strong, promoting healthy eating habits over dieting, and having realistic and healthy approaches to fitness. The women I look up to now celebrate bodies of all sizes and abilities and don't judge if you aren't a fitness fanatic. These women promote mental wellness just as much as physical wellness and know the value of loving yourself through every part of your journey. I know it can be challenging

I'm still working tirelessly to combat the toxic thought patterns I have established for myself in relation to my body and how I look. We live in a world where filters and Photoshop are the name of the game, but you shouldn't need to alter yourself for the outside world to feel beautiful inside. I mean, we all love a good picture in front of, what I like to call, a "skinny mirror" and dread that awful fitting room lighting that makes your butt dimples look like they have dimples, and that's ok. I promise you, even the most fit women in the world share these same struggles. Everyone has a little bit of insecurity in them, and we just have to work day in and day out to see ourselves as perfection creations just the way we are.

It's not easy, but with time, I promise you it's worth it. For so long, I based my worth on what men thought of me. If I was desirable in their eyes, then I was worthy. Maybe if I could dress a certain way, fit a certain size of jeans, or put on the right amount of makeup, I'd finally get the man I always dreamed of. But PSA, that crap just isn't true. At all. I've learned from experience that you have to love yourself on the inside to project your true beauty out into the world. If you believe it, those around you will see it too. Be bold. Be confident. Love every ounce of yourself in the skin you're in. And constantly strive to be 100%, unapologetically, authentically you, because we are all beautiful in our own unique ways and should celebrate it

DATING, ANXIETY AND
KNOWING YOUR WORTH

This chapter is particularly painful for me to write because this is one area in my life that is still severely lacking. I just haven't quite figured it out, and it is heartbreaking for me. From the time I was a little girl, I dreamt of how being in love would feel. I think many of us who grew up watching the fairytale princesses Disney put on the big screen may have developed some unrealistic expectations. But even as I got older, the societal messages didn't really change.

The movies and TV shows I spent hours binging as a child and adolescent were full of love stories. You had Freddie Prinze Jr. and Rachael Leigh Cook in She's All That, Corey and Topanga on Boy Meets World, Tom Hanks and Meg Ryle in You've Got Mail, and the infamous tearjerker, A Walk to Remember with Shane West and Mandy Moore. Those were just a few of my favorites, all of which fed into my developing views and expectations on true love and relationships.

When I was little, it was all about making Barbie and Ken fall in love. They'd hug, kiss, and hang out together in Barbie's Dream House. The messages I was sent told me that this romantic, fairytale love, marriage with kids scenario was precisely how life worked out for everyone, not just for my pal Barbie. My parents and the parents of my friends were all still married and living in, what I thought then, was blissful harmony. Until I reached high school, I didn't even know anyone who was a child of divorce, so I just assumed everyone got their happily ever after.

Once I reached 4th, 5th, and 6th grade, I started to see "love" stories beginning for my friends. Like I mentioned earlier in the book, my friends always had boyfriends from the time we were young, but it never really happened for me. I was always jealous and envious of their luck, wishing someone would sweep me off my feet and wondering what I needed to change to gain the attention of a boy.

As you know, in the beginning it was all about my looks. I was fat and unattractive. My friends were cute and thin. I mean, we all had other great qualities. We were smart, talented, fun, and funny. My friends and I truly had the world in our hands, we just didn't know it at the time. And really, when it came to "dating" as an adolescent, none of those deeper personal qualities mattered quite as much as how you looked.

This same pattern would follow me through middle and high school. Teenagers are savages, so it didn't get much easier as I aged. Once I got through my anorexia and was thinner, I did start to attract minimal levels of interest from men, but nothing like what my friends were receiving. I was still awkward and hadn't really developed my softer, feminine side that my friends seemed to possess. Hair, makeup, fashion, acting like a lady... I wouldn't find my way in those areas for a few more years.

Most of my friends had "long-term" relationships during middle and high school. Any type of "dating" I would be involved in was always short lived. While my friend's boyfriends made their interest public, the guys I talked to all seemed to like our relationships to be more of a secret. There weren't really any dates, hand holding or public displays of affection. My one potential relationship, which I mentioned before, ended abruptly when his ex-girlfriend tried to attack me at a school dance. Super fun times.

When it came time for prom, there was no one knocking down the door to request I be their date. I had to ask a guy friend from another school, who had a crush on one of my girlfriends, if he would be my date, because at least I knew he'd be fun. There were no slow dances for me at prom or romantic pictures taken for me to reminiscence on decades later. It was the same old, same old. Awkward, okay-looking

Carrie with the big mouth and big attitude all alone forever.

All through middle and high school, I prayed that I would find love. There was nothing more that I wanted in life than to be a girlfriend and then a wife and then a mother. With college creeping around the corner, I thought that maybe my luck would change. I was going to be in a new environment, surrounded by thousands of new people. What an exciting prospect! Perhaps, now I would stand out to someone special.

College was a little bit better. I did meet men who were attracted to me, but the situations never turned into Facebook official relationships. Y'all know what I'm talking about. It was the same thing over and over. I'd meet someone. They'd just want to come over, get drunk and Netflix and chill. Depending on the person, sometimes it'd get to a point where we'd actually meet up at the bar with our friends and act like we like each other in public.

There was one particular "relationship" that I thought would turn into more. We will call him Chris. Chris and I met through mutual friends. He didn't live in Columbus but was frequently in town visiting his best friend. At some point, there was a Facebook DM slide and we started talking. Any time he came to Columbus, we would meet up at the bars or he would come over and hang out. After a little while, I started developing feelings for him.

We continued to talk and got to the point where I would drive up to his town to see him. I had the impression that we were starting to develop an actual relationship. However, he was just taking advantage of me. At the time, I wanted to find love so badly that I didn't notice the terrible habits I had started to form.

First mistake I made was actually trusting that he wasn't talking to other girls when he was back at home. But maybe a part of me really didn't care as long as he kept talking to and spending time with me. I was always vigilantly watching my phone for his texts and would respond immediately. If he was in town, I would do everything in my power to make sure I could see him, when I really should've noticed that he could have cared less either way. I would try to lure him in with home cooked dinner and video games, because I thought that was the way to a man's heart. Keep in mind, this man never took me on a real date.

The first breaking point came for me one Valentine's Day weekend when I drove up to his town to spend time with him. His house was a two-hour drive away and it was snowing uncontrollably. Hello, Ohio weather! When I got there, he was out at the bar drunk with friends. I told him I was at his house waiting and he said he'd be back soon. This man did not come home until 2am, and I had spent the majority of my evening crying on the couch. I was livid.

Clearly, he did not give a damn about me. I had driven two hours to spend Valentine's Day weekend with him, and he didn't even have the common courtesy to stay home and hang out with me. I promptly left the next day. Over the next few weeks, he made excuses and somehow worked his way back into my life, because I had no self-confidence and was desperate for a relationship. I allowed our situation to continue on, without any improvements, until he decided to start hooking up with/dating my best friend at the time.

At that point, I was so done. I hated both of them. This moron did what he could to stay in my life, take advantage of my kindness and utilize me at his convenience until he could sweep my best friend off her feet. Once again, I had been outshined by a peer. She was thinner, more pretty and much more confident than me. The worst part was, he was 100% dedicated to her, treating her like a real girlfriend and putting in way more time and effort than he ever gave to me.

Once they broke up, Chris reached out to me and told me what a mistake he made in dating my friend and how he should've treated me better. No shit, Sherlock. I treated you like a king and got nothing in return. He tried to crawl back into my life, but I had definitely moved on. He had broken me. He fed into my complex about not being good enough and needing to change myself to be worthy of a real relationship.

About a year later, I moved to Charlotte. I was ready to kiss all those Columbus assholes goodbye and throw myself into, yet again, a new pool of people. Right before my move, I learned about dating apps. They were starting to become popular amongst people in my age group, and my college best friend had been using Match.com to go on dates. As I was planning out my move, I decided to set up a profile myself and use it to meet men in Charlotte before I got there.

My plan was to get to know people and maybe pursue a date or two once I moved down south. I had become pen pals with a few guys (anyone that's used a dating app knows what I'm talking about here), and had started to gain real interest in one in particular. Once I moved down, we continued to talk and eventually met up. He turned out to be a total douchebag, so I cut him off and was back to square one.

I continued to use Match.com until my subscription expired and then tried to set off on my own. I never liked the whole idea of dating apps to begin with. I wanted to meet someone in person the old school way and be properly courted. I wanted a fine young man to approach me, ask for my number, call me and ask me on a date. This was my ideal scenario, and I was willing to hold out for it.

Luckily for me, the group of girls I had met and begun to hang out with after my move were well connected in the Charlotte community. We went out frequently, and this allowed me to meet plenty of new friends and men. My old college ways were still alive and well, so from a romantic relationship perspective, I ended up making numerous poor decisions and never forming legitimate bonds with anyone.

Over the next two years I would go back and forth between using dating apps and trying to meet people organically when I was out with my friends. Neither tactic seemed to be working, and I was continuing to lose even more self-confidence, because my extremely attractive friends never shared my struggle. Then I began to work at Leroy Fox, and my group of friends shifted to include all my new coworkers.

These humans would become my people. After years of feeling like I never quite fit in, I finally found my tribe. We were a super fun, weirdo band of misfits, and I was so into it. After working there a while and getting to know everyone better, one of my bartender buddies kept mentioning wanting to hook me up with his friend, Kyle, because he wasn't a fan of his current girlfriend. From what I knew about Kyle, I thought there was no way I'd ever be interested. Aside from our love of the same music, I couldn't see what else we could possibly have in common. We met in passing at an EDM show my coworker and he were hosting, but that was the extent of our interaction. At least it was until a few months later.

I was out one night with my friends Jen and Tina at one of our fav bars, Mortimer's. We were grabbing some drinks and waiting on Tina's brother Vince to come meet up with us. When Vince showed up, he had Kyle in tow. I don't remember exactly how the night unfolded, but I do remember that Kyle and I went up to the bar at the same time and started chatting. It was instant chemistry. I knew right away that my coworker was onto something.

We talked for so long that night, and it seemed like only moments had passed. He got my number and we continued to talk. He was still off and on with his current girlfriend, but we talked and found time to get drinks together every now and then. We never kissed or had sex, but just continued to learn about each other for months and months.

During this time, he was getting big in the Charlotte DJ scene. I thought he was different than those other DJ guys, but I was being naive. As we spent more and more time together and dealt with all the possible ex-girlfriend drama, I thought that at some point he would want to make me his official girlfriend.

Kyle would always want to see me when I was out with friends and would come spend time with my roommate and I frequently. I would go to his place and hang out on nights he was off, and we always had the best time. Just like with my "relationship" with Chris, there were no actual dates. Outside of grabbing beers together every now and then, the majority of the time we spent together was at each other's homes. I knew I wanted more, but I liked him so much that I didn't even care.

I realize now that this was just another situation where I was a convenience. He was sleeping with random girls in the Charlotte scene, including his ex-girlfriend who he swore he hated, and my dumbass was doting on him at every moment. Regardless of how little effort he put in, I seemed to keep falling deeper and deeper. Looking back, I feel so embarrassed. I was just another dumb desperate girl.

I think by now that you've probably concluded that this is my signature move in dating. Be the dumb girl that does whatever it takes to hold on to a guy, because I'm never quite good enough to have someone trying to hold onto me. I would've done literally anything for Kyle and sometimes I did.

Once we finally kissed and got physical, we always tried to keep our relationship a secret so that no one in the group would find out. We didn't want his ex-girlfriend to find out and get upset, and unbeknownst to me, he was still seeing her. Looking back, I can see why she would feel so strongly about us being together. It was because he was giving her the idea that they were getting back together. Insanity, but not shocking.

I thought Kyle was somewhat invested in me, so I continued to allow this behavior. How blind could I be?? He was using me almost the entire time. No dates, no public displays of affection, no official relationship, nothing. He treated me so poorly sometimes, and I just let it happen because I didn't want to lose him.

This, embarrassingly, went on for years. Each year, without me knowing, this was cutting a little deeper into how I felt about myself. Still to this day I don't trust any man, which isn't entirely his fault. I don't think anyone would ever fight for me or want to keep me all his own. I assume every man is always looking for the next best thing or the next hotter girl to hook up with. How is it possible for me to find someone who would love me with my anxiety and how I look now or with my personality if he didn't?

I let men treat me the same way he did for the majority of my life, but the pain from my "relationship" with Kyle cut the deepest. At one point I finally broke. It took a few years, but he finally hurt me so bad and pissed me off so much that I cut him off completely. I pretended he no longer existed. When I saw him, I looked right through him as if he were a ghost.

Months later, he brought this up to me. He knew how badly he hurt me and now that the tables were turned, he was the one hurting. A part of me knew he had true feelings for me, but instead of being led by his heart, he was led by his immaturity and bad decisions and maybe was starting to regret it.

After being ignored by me for months, he finally started to apologize. Eventually he sent me a long Facebook message of all the terrible things he had done, acknowledged them, and asked for my forgiveness. At this point, he'd been blocked in my phone for quite some time, so this is how we had to communicate. Once I received the message and marinated on it for a bit, I decided to forgive him. But I forgave him for ME, not for him. Hating him was so toxic that I had to give it up. From here we started to form a friendship. We are still friends to this day, and I have completely forgiven him.

He is incredibly supportive and has even mentioned us trying to date properly, which would not work out at this point in my life. I'm really proud of how he has grown as a person, because after me he made some really poor choices in actual girlfriends who turned out to be psycho. I think he eventually realized how great of a relationship we could've had and just how much he missed out on.

Our "relationship" took a serious toll on my already damaged self-image. Hearing that he regretted his decisions and wished we could turn things around didn't make me feel any better about myself. I had this vision of hearing those words and instantly feeling better about myself. More worthy of love and perfect just how I am, but that's not reality. I'm thankful for how far he and I have come and am so grateful to have him in my life, but it makes me sad to look at the path that brought us here.

These are only two detailed examples of a long list I could share. I've already talked about Brad, so tack that one on, too. The point in sharing these stories is to demonstrate how the toxic narrative I'd written for myself about relationships led to seriously damaging consequences. I had been convinced for so long that to find love I needed to be tall, thin, and beautiful. As you already know, I had serious body image issues and they were detrimental when it came to finding love.

I also felt like I needed to be perfect in all other ways. I needed to be fun, sweet, funny, successful, properly educated, knowledgeable about all sports, like the right music, hang out at the right places, dress a certain way, etc. My list of personal expectations was endless and completely and utterly unreasonable, but I didn't see it that way. I honestly believed that the only women that found love were absolutely flawless, but I was terribly misinformed. It took years to finally realize that I was more than the sum of my flaws and worthy of love just as I am.

Worse than the expectations I had set for myself, was the way I allowed men to disrespect me and treat me as second rate. Because I displayed no self-respect or self-confidence, I got that in return. Time and time again I allowed men to walk all over me while I bent over backwards for them. Because I so desperately wanted to be in love, I would do anything to keep a man even if it meant sacrificing myself. My heart, my time, my mental health, my money. I had developed these patterns of behavior that formed into habits without me even thinking about it, and I would allow them to continue for nearly two decades.

Because of my unfortunate luck with dating, I would frequently get depressed about my inability to find a mate. There were numerous occasions where I would find myself wine drunk on the couch at home with my two roommates crying about how I'd never find love. Lynn and Kiersten heard the worst of it and would try to soothe my broken heart. Other friends would always ask me how I was still single, because they thought I was such a great catch. While that made me feel good, I felt like they were either just saying it because they were my friends or it was true, which made me feel even more confused about my inability to meet someone.

Other friends would try to reassure me that I'd find a partner, because I would be the best girlfriend and wife, but would always lead with the annoying, bullshit clichés that would really grind my gears. "You'll find love when the time is right." "It'll happen when you least expect it." "It's just not the right time for you." "It'll happen when it's meant to happen." It got to the point where I would start the conversation and let them know not to give me the cliché bullshit of "when the time is right" because it would drive me nuts. Eventually they always landed on "I just know it will happen for you, because of_____...." pointing out some quality of mine they admired.

I greatly appreciate all of my friend's kind words and overwhelming support I've received over the years. One or another of them have always been there when I've been deeply hurt, wrapping me in their arms or sending me long messages filled with love and encouragement. They've helped me break away from toxic relationships and remind me of my worth. And while I should've been working to gain this strength and wisdom on my own, it took several stern discussions and friends pushing me to expect and require more for myself to finally lead me to a healthier place.

As I gained more respect for myself, or at least thought I had, my already extensive list of requirements in a partner grew more outrageous. It's kind of ironic, I guess, because I want someone to love me as I am, flaws and all, but expect perfection in a partner. Honestly, until writing this paragraph, I never thought of it that way. (Woohoo! See folks, continual self-discovery, and learning.) Regardless, my laundry list of non-negotiables got worse over time. I considered it "not settling", but as the list got longer, the dating pool got smaller.

When I was younger, I was more superficial. You had to be a tall, dark, handsome, very fit bad boy and love to party and adventure. Not surprisingly, this led to hanging out with a lot of douchebags, plain and simple. I spent a lot of time at the gym, at one point working there, so I had easy access to this type of dudes. They were great for going out to the clubs on the weekend, but worthless beyond that. Most of them were personal trainers, employees at the gym or bartenders, all of which were disrespectful womanizers.

As I reached my mid to late 20's, I started having slightly less superficial expectations, but still, the list was somewhat unreasonable. Now I wanted someone tall, dark, nice looking, into health and wellness, college educated, solid career, close to their family, have a lot of friends, kind, empathetic, generous, into traveling, interested in more than partying and not a superficial prat. If I'm being honest, the list didn't stop there, and I considered many of the traits listed to be non-negotiables in a partner.

Obviously, if you meet someone in person, you will only get surface level details. You see what they look like, might get details on their education or career and possibly some hobbies or shared interests, but the thing about meeting someone in person is that you can tell if you have chemistry right away. Personally, when meeting potential suitors in person, I am much more open minded in terms of what I'm attracted to and who I may be interested in long-term. The problem is, quite a bit of dating is now done online or with phone apps.

Because of my anxiety, I have stopped going out as frequently as I had in the past. And not that I was having any luck before in the dating world, but this certainly added an element of complexity to meeting someone. My fear of having a panic attack or feeling anxious while drinking has turned me into a homebody. Therefore, I turn to the apps, Bumble and Hinge being the most frequently used.

While using apps can be great for some people, I find they enable me to become more and more picky in what I think is acceptable in a partner. You can see height, activity level, college education, job and so on. I've also found that men struggle a bit with creating a profile... profiles with all gym/shirtless selfies, profiles where you can't even tell which person it is, profiles where they're wearing sunglasses in all the photos, photos from angles that you never want to look at human's face... you get it. They might be perfectly normal, attractive, sweet men, but lawd, the profiles are a mess. Because your profile is the gateway to gaining that right swipe, I feel like they could spruce it up a bit...but who am I to talk?

Because of my luck in dating and severely lacking trust in men, I don't take the apps seriously. I usually only swipe when I'm bored and need entertainment or one of my married friends wants to see what single people go through on the app. I mean, I don't know if you have found yourself in this position, but I might swipe left so many times that I run out of people before I even find one that's a possibility. I know I'm not alone, because my girlfriends have experienced this too. If you don't actually scroll through the profiles and read the answers, you can lose track of time swipe, swipe, swiping, and next thing you know 20 minutes have gone by and you have yet to find someone.

Now let's jump to actually finding someone who meets my criteria. If it's Bumble, I'm forced to message first, which I hate. If it's Hinge, and I actually match them, then at least they have to do the beginning leg work. Because of my past self-confidence issues, I wrongfully believe that if they don't message me first, they're not interested. I have learned over time that men are just as nervous as women, but that hasn't helped me become more confident and assertive.

Once a conversation becomes initiated, here's where the real fun begins. What is this conversation going to be like? Usually it's a "Hey. How are you?" type of thing and then dies off after three or four exchanges with the person. If we actually have a more meaningful conversation, perhaps it will go on for a few days. If our conversation is going really well, sometimes we will move to texting. That typically doesn't last long either, because I'll be too anxious to actually meet up, they'll say something off putting or I'll talk to them about my anxiety and they'll run.

I know I'll probably catch some shit for this, but I'm just trying to be honest here. More times than not, I get bored and let the conversation die off. Dating apps make it too easy to jump from one thing to the next, bypassing the need to pursue deeper connections, because if you don't feel something right away, there's 100's of more options out there. Dating in this day and age involves a lot of "onto the next thing," which I hate but also participate in. It's awful, but it's reality. On numerous occasions, I've wished we could go back to simpler times with more focus on putting time and effort into your mate and allowing feelings to develop over time, but that's just not where we are anymore.

My anxiety also keeps me from wanting to go on a date, because I'm convinced every man is superficial, possesses zero empathy or has ulterior motives. The combination of my boredom and anxiety, lands me back at square one, disgruntled and down on myself because I can't meet someone. It's a depressing cycle that occurs over and over again. I know what you're thinking: "This girl is insane and it's abundantly clear why she is single." Go easy on me folks, I'm still learning.

The problem is, I am very afraid. I'm afraid of having my heart broken, of embarrassing myself because of my anxiety, of someone abandoning me because of my anxiety, of someone leaving if I gain a pound or two, of being cheated on or of not being appreciated for my 100% authentic self. This fear is my greatest hindrance and also one of the main reasons that none of my app convos lead to dates. The other major reason is because I think that everyone is a kidnapper or murderer, but I listen to a LOT of My Favorite Murder and Morbid. This girl is trying to #StaySexyandDon'tGetMurdered. On the other side of this fear is my fear of never meeting someone, never falling in love, never knowing what it's like to share this type of special relationship with another human and never getting married. Two very distinct sets of fears, same crippling outcome.

Over time these fears have grown, and are byproducts of personal experience, the experience of loved ones or societal statistics on dating and marriage. The other dominant factor has been my continual battle with anxiety. From what you've already read, you can see how this condition has, at times, been crippling, especially the end of 2019 and beginning of 2020. During that time period, I lost a lot of faith in myself and faith in my ability to maintain friendships and meet my soulmate. I felt I had to "fix" my anxiety problem before I would be worthy of love... I still feel that way a lot of the time.

Allowing this narrative to take up space in my head has led to absolute heartbreak. My therapist has watched me break down on many occasions, because of my fear of the anxiety never improving and fear of never finding a partner. Despite the number of conversations we have had on these two matters, I still can't find it in me to switch my toxic thought patterns. A part of me is petrified that my anxiety will continue to worsen or never improve, and with that, I feel no one will ever be able to love me.

Why would anyone want to deal with someone like me? Someone

with body image issues, self-confidence issues and worst of all, anxiety. It's too much for me to handle sometimes, so why should I expect that someone else would extend me that courtesy? In order to be lovable, I need to be happy, bubbly, positive Polly all the time. Those are the types of girls that have husbands, not worried, whiny, negative Nancy. I mean, I'm not always a negative Nancy, but mental health disorders can really make you feel some type of way sometimes and you have no control over that. How could I expect someone to understand, and dare I say, embrace me as I am during those moments?

I know this all sounds preposterous, but my brain's been wired to believe this nonsense. The perplexing part is that deep inside, I know I'm a catch. A teeny, angelic voice inside my head tells me that I'm worthy of love and have so much to offer, but the gremlin that coexists inside there frequently takes over and reminds me that I'm more of a burden than I'm worth. The power struggle between light and dark is exhausting, I tell ya. If you've ever felt this way, I'm deeply sorry. I know how hard it is and how damaging it can be to your heart and soul.

I can also tell you, you are worth everything and more. Anyone would be lucky to have you in their life. You are so much more than your mental health disorder, your past experiences, and your fears. You deserve all the love and respect that exists in this universe and beyond. Why is it so hard to tell ourselves these messages, but offering them to a loved one, or even a stranger, is so simple?

We need to learn to bestow the same kindness offered to others on ourselves. We need to speak kindlier, love ourselves more openly and embrace who we are as individuals. We need to recognize our worth, knowing we are greater than the sum of our flaws, and the most fundamental piece of advice I could ever give, never settle for less than we deserve. If you feel for even the slightest moment that you are losing part of yourself to cater to a partner, get out. Do not allow yourself to become a puppet on behalf of someone else's pleasure, because there are way too many fish in the sea for that crap.

Respect yourself enough to hold out for an equal, someone who is working just as hard as you are to be the best person they can be. When coming up with a list of non-negotiables in a mate, make sure that list includes kindness (and I mean kindness to everyone, not just their friends and family. This also includes animals.), empathy, loyalty, honesty, respect, intelligence, motivation, and patience. This is the list I should be using, not the crazy one I shared above. These are fundamental values in a grade-A, decent human being.

And while you are out there looking for that perfect match, know that perfection isn't real. You have flaws, so will they, but a good partnership is one where you honor the value of the whole person without dwelling on their imperfections. Mostly importantly, never give up. Stay positive, send your desire out into the universe/God, and whole-heartedly have faith that it will happen. I've spent an embarrassing amount of time in therapy working through this topic and will continue to do so until I believe it just as much as I'm encouraging you to believe.

Oh, and if being in a relationship and getting married isn't for you, more power to you. I honestly believe some of the happiest people are the ones that have learned to be happy by themselves. Learning to sit with yourself and love the special relationship you have created within is something to be cherished. No one should feel the need to fit the stereotypical American dream. Having a partner, house, and 2.5 kids all before the age of 30 is whack, and we need to normalize the reality that extends the net of possibility so much wider.

We are all divine beings, created by our higher powers and placed on this earth to love and be loved. Repeat this every day until it feels like your truth. God knows, I need this reminder more often than I'm willing to admit. And remember, no matter what happens in your love life, the most important love you will ever receive, comes from within. That's the only form of unconditional love for which we should go to battle and hold onto for dear life. And like my girl Robin Arzon (Oh hey, PeloPeeps!), hold your head high queens and kings, because that's the only way to keep your crown on straight. Remember, we are all royalty.

Note: If you are experiencing abuse or violence in your relationship or are in a situation where you feel unsafe but cannot navigate your way out, inform someone you trust and/or call the National Domestic Violence Hotline at 1-800-799-SAFE or use their online chat feature at www.TheHotline.org. Take responsibility for your own wellbeing and love yourself enough to get out.

LEARNING TO SAY NO

As a "yes (wo)man", it is particularly challenging for me to say no to anything, even when saying yes will cause me deep distress. Unfortunately, this affects all areas of my life, personal and professional. For me, saying no feels like letting down whomever is asking something of me, which those of you who share this plight may understand.

Because I hold myself to such a high standard in the workplace and suffer from overachiever syndrome, the word "no" really isn't in my professional vocabulary. I also like to play teacher's pet and be the favorite, which creates its own host of issues. Living this type of existence, creates unhealthy thought patterns of which I am not proud.

When someone else is praised for performing highly, and I am not, I feel a sense of jealous rage building up inside. Then I start a barrage of self-deprecating internal discussions and occasionally with other people. My work buddy has been the recipient of these chats on a number of occasions. I want him to succeed. He deserves every ounce of praise he gets and then some, because he is an absolute rockstar employee and coworker, but if he gets a compliment and I don't, yikes.

If I receive review comments on something or make a tiny mistake that a manager has to fix, I lose my mind. This has privately driven me to tears in the past. "How could I be making these mistakes? I'm the senior. I need to outperform everyone." When someone is given an extra responsibility that wasn't offered to me, I immediately rummage through the filing cabinet in my head for reasons why that could have possibly happened. It's ridiculous and exhausting.

The sweet, kind natured and loving part of my personality wants everyone to succeed. The envious, jealous, green gremlin side wants to be the trophy employee at all times, no matter what. This, my friends, is what drives me to be a yes (wo)man.

When asked to pick up a task, train someone, review something, participate in an extra project, help another team or any other God forsaken addition to my responsibility list is requested, I say yes. Every. Single. Time. A sense of duty compels me to say yes, as does my psychotic expectations of myself. And God forbid someone asks to take something off my plate or tell me they're reassigning one of my tasks to another person. No, no, no. That sends me down a whole different spiral. "Why are they taking this from me? Am I underperforming? Do they think I can't handle it?" "WHY do they think I can't handle it? Who is performing more highly than I am?"

Oh, and training someone on a task that only I know how to do? Nope, don't want to do that. I want to feel completely indispensable. This stems from another one of my irrational fears about being fired at any moment. Regardless of my value in the workplace, this can realistically happen anyway depending on the job market or the economic state of the company, so worrying about it ain't helping shit. It's making me look like a selfish brat and feel like a terrible human being. I've never actually said no or didn't provide 110% when training anyone, but the gremlin... he's inside there.

The weird part is, mentoring, training people, being a "buddy" and being available to coworkers 24/7 for questions are job functions I LOVE. They make me so happy. When asked to train or mentor, I am always one of the first to volunteer. I love teaching people and guiding them to greatness, so it's odd that it can so negatively impact me at any given time, but my gremlin has a mind of its own. Stupid little bugger.

All of these scenarios have occurred more than once. I'll never forget, long ago when one of my managers had a serious talk with me about always agreeing to any and everything requested of me. She told me that, as a leader, she would respect me more if I set boundaries for myself and occasionally said no instead of constantly saying yes. I had honestly never even considered that before. I can't say it's necessarily impacted my thought patterns or behavior quite yet, but that conversation will always hover in the back of my mind.

More recently, I did try to take up for myself (and our whole team, actually) when we were already engrossed in off-quarter projects and were assigned another time-consuming task unexpectedly. The manager's response was to try to take work off my plate. I was immediately offended. Like big time. Enough so that I set up an hour-long call with boss to go through my schedule and prove I was capable.

Before our call, we briefly discussed the issue. She also told me she would respect me more if I took on less but performed those tasks to near perfection than to take on 15 different items and give them 75-80%. My overarching issue is that I want to take on 15 tasks and also perform at 100% consistently, which isn't always possible. She also reminded me that the volume of projects isn't always indicative of the complexity of the tasks at hand. While, yes, I did have a large volume of projects, they were also more time consuming and in-depth than those assigned to other teammates. Her saying that made me realize that, okay, maybe sometimes it was alright to allow others to step in and help and that delegating smaller tasks to other teammates may free up time for more burdensome assignments, allowing me to perform more highly and keep my mental state intact.

I'm still learning to allow others to shine next to me instead of standing in the shadow of my light and to share learning responsibilities without feeling like my position or reputation is in jeopardy. My true soul wants everyone to succeed, especially my current coworkers who are all incredibly hardworking human beings and great friends. I recently admitted this to one of my main gals at work and she was so sweet about it. A sense of relief came over me after putting it out there. She didn't judge me or try to make me feel guilty about having those feelings, and she acknowledged how it must be difficult to experience these conflicting thoughts.

Sometimes the best way to tackle difficult internal experiences is to be honest with yourself and with others. Acknowledge, "Okay, this is not an admirable trait, so I would not like to possess this trait any longer." Then whenever those thoughts and feelings arise, talk them down. Beating yourself up is counterproductive. Put your energy into changing the narrative. "Just because others shine, doesn't mean I can't shine too." Remember, our light is brighter when we shine together. I genuinely believe that.

And stop saying yes to everything. People really will respect you more when you take up for yourself and your well-being. Learning to say no, happily say no, will give you room to breathe. If you notice you're working hours later than your peers or managers and feel like you can never keep up or catch up, evaluate what is on your plate. And don't be afraid to ask for help. From a co-worker, from a manager, whoever. Respect yourself enough to speak up. It's not benefitting anyone for you to wait until the last minute to realize you cannot complete an assignment timely. You're putting yourself and your team in a bad position. Take responsibility for your own schedule. Where you see conflicts, set up time to speak with your manager or a leader you trust. I promise you, they want you to succeed as much as you want you to succeed, because success of one is success of many. I'm sure you've heard the saying "You're only as strong as your weakest link." Well, it's true.

If you're not in a corporate role, this applies to you, as well. If you're a stay-at-home mom and you need a break, ask a friend to come babysit, even if it's for you to take a nap. If you're in a restaurant job and you have personal obligations such as school or family needs, talk to coworkers or your boss so that resources can be reallocated. If you're a burnt-out fitness instructor, ask a teammate to step in. I'm sure they'd be happy for the bonus income and face time with clients. Sometimes all that is what saying no looks like. And if you can't do any of the above, get you a new job quick, because that isn't sustainable for anyone. At least not anyone who wants to keep their sanity in check.

Saying no doesn't just apply to the workplace. In fact, saying no outside of work is more difficult for me. I'm blessed to have a team that feels like family, so what I'm about to discuss does occasionally bleed into my professional life. Social no's just feel harder. Saying no to a friend or family member can leave an ugly sense of unnecessary guilt. This becomes increasingly difficult the more social circles you run in and the closer you are (literally and figuratively) with family.

I'll start with family. Just because you are a blood relative of someone does not obligate you to say yes to everything they ask. You don't HAVE to babysit their child. You don't HAVE to come to a gathering they're putting together. You don't HAVE to lend them money, etc. I haven't personally encountered these scenarios, but I know plenty of friends that have.

If someone is asking for your time and you don't have time to give, politely decline. "I'm sorry, I'd love to help, but I have XYZ responsibility to take care of during that time." or "I'm sorry, but I have prior obligations to fulfil, but if I'm available next time, I'd love to help." And if you just really wouldn't ever love to help, then you shouldn't be feeling bad in the first place. If it's to babysit, "I'm sorry, but I really don't trust myself alone with a child. I don't have enough experience and want your child to have fun and be safe." If it's a task around the house, "I'm sorry, but I just don't think I would do as good of a job as (insert person you think would be a better resource)." And you know what, screw the "I'm sorry" because you shouldn't be sorry for declining. Say what you need to say and get on with it.

If it's a gathering someone put together, just politely decline and explain you have important prior obligations to attend or that you have a personal agenda to contend with. It's no one's business what you do in your free time and if that is just sitting on your couch in the dark, huddled under a blanket for hours at a time, great! Shoot them a text from your blanket fort and keep it moving.

If it's money, then simple. "I'd love to be able to help you, but I have my own bills to pay this month." Don't get yourself in a financial bind to help anyone. This applies to family, friends, acquaintances, or friends. No one is responsible for your financial obligations but you, and this applies to everyone, including the people asking for money. If you can afford it and know the person will pay you back, then go for it. But so many times, I've seen friends lend money and never see it again. Money can break relationships. I've seen friendships crumble over money. That person that was your "best friend" when they needed

$500 has now magically disappeared and blocked you on social media … yeah, be careful who you lend money to, family or friend. And if you're going to do it, lend with the mindset of never getting it back, because it's always a possibility.

All the above really applies to friends and family, not just a blood relative, but where I really struggle on the friend spectrum is social events. I used to be a huge partier. I went out six or seven days a week and drank my face off with my friends. We would meet at someone's house early, pregame, go to the bars, dance the night away, sometimes after party, and I'd end up passed out in bed anywhere between 3am and 5am. Not anymore, hunny. Those days are long gone.

Now, I'm a homebody turned super hermit by my worsening anxiety over the years. An enormous part of me does not want to say no to friends, because to maintain friendships, you need to interact with the people outside of that 3x6in area of your cell phone. The other part does not want to be out, especially any time past 9pm and doesn't want to feel obligated to drink alcohol.

My anxiety partially made me this way, but I don't think it's all bad. I was definitely drinking way too much before and spending too much money for a few hours of enjoyment, but I do miss being carefree. Feeling this way does have challenges though. When friends invite me out for drinks or to go out or to do dinner at like 9pm, I really don't want to. I also despise being out on a "school night" aka after work. After work I want to decompress, cook dinner, and read, not get home at 11pm or midnight and then have to struggle to fall asleep. Not cool.

Because I'm in accounting, I could easily blame work for missing literally anything. Don't want to get drinks after work? Sorry, I have to work late today. Don't want to attend a party on the weekend? Sorry, we are in busy season, and my manager is expecting me to be online. Sometimes this was true, many times it was not. I tried to stop using this excuse because I deeply fear karma. One day, she's going to bite me in the butt, and I'll be working until 10pm every day. No. Thank you.

It's also not cool to lie to your friends. Every now and again, if you need to tell a white lie to get out of doing something, that's fine. We all do it, but I think honesty goes a lot further. You don't want to continually decline and make up excuses, because eventually they may stop asking. Then you're left feeling alone and unwanted by the people you care about most. This is also more challenging when you are in multiple friend groups that can't easily be melded together.

I find what works best for me in these scenarios is to try to plan your own events or meet ups, so that you can see as many friends at once as possible and potentially foster some new friendships. Maybe instead of heading to a small speakeasy for drinks with one group, suggest hitting a brewery where there's more space and room for people to roam and socialize. Plus, many of those places allow you to bring pets, and who doesn't like to bond over cute dogs?

You could also organize a little get together at your house, go out to eat or suggest attending an upcoming local event where people may come and go as they please. Then you are in control of the situation and who you'd like to see. If you know there are certain people who won't mesh well, then see them separately. By doing this, you may even save yourself over time, realizing you have some toxic relationships in your circle that don't play well with others and can start to distance yourself.

By stepping back from the party scene, I realized that there were relationships that were not feeding my soul. I wanted to be surrounded by loving, caring individuals who loved me for me in and outside of the bar. I think we have all been there. You have your real friends and your party friends. Some of those were synonymous, and I have developed and maintained, what I believe to be, lifelong relationships with those individuals. Others fell off because they did not grow in ways I was growing. I no longer want to be surrounded by the "cool" kids or most popular on the Charlotte scene. I want to be surrounded by wholesome, hardworking, inspirational, kind, compassionate adults that push me to be better every day. THOSE are the people you say yes to, time and time again.

Another tactic I like to use when I have to say no or am just not interested in saying yes, is to offer a counter plan. Because alcohol isn't a big part of my life anymore, I like to find activities to do that don't involve drinking. If friends want to go out for drinks later in the evening, I suggest alternative options for us to see each other at a later date. Using this tactic, I've never had someone turn me down.

I have a passion for fitness, so I frequently suggest wellness dates with friends. Many of my friends love this. Yoga is always a good one to start with, because it's approachable for everyone at any fitness level. If you have friends that are more athletic, find a local boutique fitness studio and go support them! Shout out to my favorite gals over at West Kept Secret in Charlotte, always keeping in fun, funky and fresh and slowly killing me with cardio! Doing these dates has brought even more wonderful humans into my life, so give it a try. When you're doing something you feel passionate about with other people that share your passion, that's how you create lasting bonds.

My friend Amber is one of the best examples. She was a contractor in my office that happened to sit across from me. We would chat on a regular basis and formed a surface level friendship. After a few coffee dates, we started communicating more and learned we shared a passion for fitness and reading. Now we go to yoga classes together, get lunch, grab coffee, check out restorative wellness studios, etc. She has become someone I trust with my whole life and who I admire for the assiduous, beautiful, inspiring soul she shares with me.

For the pals in your life who'd rather sip than sweat, suggest dinner or brunch at a time that suits you. Don't want to meet up at 8 or 9pm for dinner? Suggest making reservations for 7 or 7:30pm. Don't want to stay out late but want to see your gals? Go to lunch or brunch. Find a patio and grab some drinks while it's sunny outside and catch up on the latest gossip. Suggest a nail appointment or trip to the mall. Heck, I've even invited friends over to sit around in pjs and watch movies. Or offer to go over to their place. "Hey, I'm slammed this week and feeling a little burnt out, how about I stop by on XYZ day and we catch up?" Works every time.

And honestly, if life is getting the best of you and you're all tuckered out, just simply say no. Telling people you're tired and need alone time is perfectly fine and should require zero excuses. If anyone tries to peer pressure or make you feel apologetic about staying at home, maybe they're not the right type of friend for you.

Different personalities have different priorities and interests. Some people can go, go, go, and thrive in that world. And some of us want to be home in our oversized sweats with whatever book came in our latest Book of the Month box, a sweet little gray kitty in our laps and a cup of coffee (Venti, iced, decaf Americano if you're like me). And you know what, neither should feel ashamed. Everyone has a breaking point. We all reach it at different periods in our lives, which means everyone can relate to that "leave me the heck alone" feeling.

Saying no means guarding your mental health, and that's what this book is all about. There's no need to get FOMO or feel left out when you turn someone down and chill on your couch. There will always be a next time. YOU can create the next time under your terms. The ones that love you will get it. The ones that don't, well, screw 'em! Do what's best for you, be honest about it and find the balance that fills you with the most joy.

Carrie Thompson

COMFORT ZONES

I think staying in our comfort zones is one of the contributors to staying stuck in our anxiety and/or not seeing the forward progress we'd prefer. The only way to change or progress through anxiety is by letting go of control, but when we stay in our comfort zones, we feel more like we are in control. When you are stuck in this pattern, you need to ask yourself, "What is the reason that I want to change?" What am I willing to do to make the changes?" "What am I giving up by staying stagnant?"

My therapist always told me that when you've come to the realization that you've surpassed your threshold for discomfort, you are more likely to start making the necessary changes to improve your situation. At that point you're so far down the hole that you will do anything to get out. However, even when I reached that point, I was still afraid to leave my comfort zone. In my mind, I was making the changes and doing the work, but in reality, I wasn't giving it 100%.

I think a lot of us fall into that trap over and over. I spent more time in my head thinking about what I wanted to change and about how I was failing to make those changes instead of moving forward and doing the work. I've just now started to sit with the discomfort and see where it takes me. It's taken me years in therapy to get to this point, and still to this day it takes a lot to push me past my comfort threshold and to the point of change.

Change is scary, plain, and simple. Personally, when thinking about the plan forward, I get caught up in thinking about what could go wrong or that by doing something differently, I will actually worsen an already painful situation. The crappy part about that is, I may be right, but we have no way of knowing that if we don't try. On the flipside, we could land ourselves in a much more promising situation, but without a little courage, we'll never find out. This is where you must evaluate the options based on the information at hand, make a choice and take a leap of faith to see where you'll ultimately land.

If you really want to get serious about it, make a list of the things that you want to change. Consider what you risk losing if you never take the first step. Consider what your life would be like without making those changes, and even more so, imagine what your life would be like if you did make the changes and they worked out in your favor. If you're in therapy, I suggest going through this process with your therapist, because they will be an unbiased individual that can help hold you accountable and act as a sounding board as you set up your goals. At least this has proven true for me.

If you don't have a therapist, I highly recommend seeking one out and/or confiding in someone you look up to that is levelheaded and has a stable life. These individuals will be your accountability buddies, people you can lean on when the plan isn't quite working out in your favor or people to consult when you see an opportunity to change your course. If you're really lucky, you'll also have those certain individuals in your life who know you better than you know yourself or at least well enough to help you test your limits. I encouraged you to identify who those people are for you, talk openly about your struggles and goals, and make a point to spend a lot of quality time with them when possible.

For me, my friends Lynn and Mikey just get it. They may not fully understand where my head is or what I'm going through, but they respect my boundaries and help protect my mental wellbeing. Because they are so understanding of my anxiety, it's nuances, potential situations that make me tick, etc., I am more comfortable doing activities a little out of my ordinary when in their presence. They were the first people who could convince me to go on a trip without my family nearby after my mental breakdown the prior December. They got me to come away for a mountain weekend to spend time with friends and new acquaintances.

Because of the pandemic, it was a pure necessity to get away to somewhere with fresh air, trees, nature, mountains and just disconnect from reality. The Stay-At-Home order in North Carolina had kept us cooped up inside for weeks, and everyone needed a mental health refresh and break from staring at the four walls inside our homes. I missed my friends and they missed me. We felt that with a small group of people who had been quarantining and taking necessary precautions, that it would be fine to go.

It took a bit of convincing for me, because at the time my anxiety still largely fluctuated from day to day and week to week. After dwelling on it for far too long, I decided that I would be mad at myself if I didn't go. I'd be missing out on some potentially incredible memories if I catered to my own unnecessary fears and stayed home. Everyone else was planning to go up Friday night that week, but I had a hair appointment that Saturday morning, so I went up Saturday afternoon. Luckily, my dad offered to drive up with me, because 2 ½ hours alone in the car still seemed overwhelming, and after deciding to go, I didn't want anything to hinder my decision.

The trip wasn't all rainbows and butterflies. I had very anxious moments, but I pushed through. I was really upset that I couldn't just be "normal" and relaxed like everyone else. I couldn't drink and party like I used to and be carefree, but as I reflect back on those moments, I'm proud of myself for sticking it out and enjoying myself the best I could. I mean, you can only sit inside your house for so long, with your only "social outings" being to the grocery store or the Starbucks and Chik-fil-a drive-throughs. Contact with your beloved family and friends, coupled with a ton of good conversation and laughs, is a good part of what gets you through everyday life, especially during a pandemic. The trip was worth every second and gave me confidence to continue pushing forward on this difficult journey.

The other person that I'm so grateful for on this "recovery" journey is my girl Gina. She knows how to push me harder than some of my other friends but is unwavering in her love and support. When things really get uncomfortable, she can switch from challenging my boundaries to helping me come back down to earth and get grounded. We were roomies in college and have stayed close friends over the years. We have had some serious ups and downs, primarily because of my anger and jealousy issues, but because of her heart of gold, we have maintained a strong bond.

Three quarters of the way through the apocalyptic year that was 2020, this beautiful soul got with my parents to give me the greatest surprise ever. She decided to fly into Charlotte and surprise me. They had been planning her surprise visit for a few weeks, and I was completely in the dark. Then one random Friday night, when my mom and I had planned a girls only sleepover, my dad insisted on stopping by to pick up some dinner around 9:30pm. It seemed a little fishy, but my dad does weird stuff frequently and honestly, I thought he was just jealous of mom and wanted to come see my cat. After a few minutes of him messing around with my cat and acting like he was getting food out of my fridge, I hear my front door open. My living room has a direct view of the front door, so I leaned over off the couch to see who the hell was entering my house so late, and OH EM GEE! IT WAS GINA!

I was exhausted that day and was basically in trance when I saw her. I couldn't believe my eyes and was left speechless. My family loves this girl, so we were all full of hugs and smiles. Now, this all sounds fantastic but remember, I'm an OCD, Type A, "everything has to be planned out minute to minute" person, whose whole schedule for the weekend just got thrown for a loop. I had actually planned to write a few chapters of this book that weekend, clean my house, run errands and get a massage. Being that I had gotten a bit discouraged and some writers block earlier in the week, I was really depending on the weekend to catch up and now that was out the door. This had been the first time since my complete breakdown in December that my agenda was being threatened, and I could feel the anxiety creeping in.

The first night she was there I couldn't sleep because of excitement AND anxiety. My elation at her surprising me with a visit was being hammered on by my rigidity and anxiety. I tried to soothe myself but spent the night tossing and turning. The next day I woke up and gave myself a reality check. One of my best friends had just flown in all the way from Chicago for ME. I was being an enormous brat about it just because I like to stick to a schedule. I decided that moment that the schedule was out the window. I really had no reason to even feel this way to begin with, because she told me she just wanted to see me and that we could do my normal routine anyway. But that wasn't good enough. I wanted us to make some damn good memories and was determined to turn my mindset around and show her a fantastic time.

The first day was very relaxed. She ran some errands with me, and then we spent some time with my parents, because she's been a part of our little family for over ten years. We stayed up later than I normally do, but that night I slept like a rock. The next day when I woke up, I knew the world was not ready for what we were about to bring to the table. Sunday Funday, at its finest, was about to go down. We had brunch plans with Lynn and Mikey and then a day of adventure afterwards.

After getting ready, we headed to brunch for Gina to meet my little crew. Gina and I took it back to our days of living in Columbus together and jammed out to some 2000's rap music on the drive. When we finally arrived, late of course because getting ready with your bestie just goes that way sometimes, introductions couldn't have gone better. Everyone melded perfectly, which just added to the positive energy I was already feeling about the day. After brunch we did a little tour of some of the group's favorite Southend Charlotte spots to give her a taste of our usual adventures. The first stop was Zeppelin, which is one of my favorite places to eat and drink in Charlotte. She loved the drink menu and got to meet some more of my friends. Next was Leroy Fox, because of course she had to see my bar job and taste some of our delicious apps and cocktails. Then we headed to Gin Mill. I hadn't been there in forever, but we were just rolling with whatever came to mind.

At this point, it was 3pm and we had been drinking since noon. I hardly drink anymore, we are talking one glass of wine a week or so, and I was starting to get a bit anxious about it. I started getting in my own head and felt the anxious body symptoms coming on. I was feeling grouchy, fidgety and my heart rate was climbing. I sat down and explained to her and Mikey what was going on. This led to a heart-to-heart with them about my anxiety and how I feel like a burden to my friends and family and completely unworthy of their incredible friendship. Tears were shed, but then we moved on.

Gina pushed me to be strong and convinced me to stay out longer. Just seeing her joy, the bonds she was forming with my friends and the fun she was having was enough of an argument without her having to speak any words. I wasn't about to ruin her visit and our time together by catering to my anxious ways. I decided to just stop drinking, get some food, and relax. We went to one last spot, where she and Mikey got food and finally went home around 9:30. This was huge for me. I hadn't stayed out that late in forever. When we got home, we stayed up talking until 12:30am and then finally went to bed.

This may seem like an ordinary day for many people, but for me this was serious progress. Even if I felt uncomfortable and anxious, I stuck it out. I'm so grateful she gave me that opportunity and pushed me past my own limit. She also imparted some good anxiety wisdom on me that evening. Recently, she had gone through a similar situation with anxiety after never having experienced it before. She was working in an extremely toxic work environment, and it was driving her to a dark place. After finally switching to a new career, her whole mindset and life turned around.

Her point of telling me all this, in more detail than I'm offering here, was to encourage me and remind me that my current circumstances could improve. She told me that I might not be stuck in this rut for the rest of my life. This is one of my fears, you know. Probably my biggest fear. I am afraid that I will always have unpredictable anxiety and anxious tendencies. She blatantly said, "That is the difference between me and you. You are afraid you will stay this way forever, and I knew it was temporary. I knew that through some lifestyle modifications, I could change the way I felt."

I can't say that it changed my mind on the spot because I'm stubborn and set in my ways, but it opened a window of possibility. That wonderful Sunday, she had challenged me in more ways than she ever could've imagined. She challenged the way I lived and the way I thought. She tried to push me past the limitations and boundaries I had drawn for myself. Other than my therapist, no one can talk to me that way or really make me think. I will never forget that weekend and just how much she gave me by surprising me with a visit and continuing to show me her unwavering love and support.

These stories are examples of what I mentioned above. Surround yourself with a positive, supportive, and uplifting network of humans. If you are surrounded by friends, colleagues, family members and a community who is allowing you to be complacent, you need to reevaluate what is going on. Know your worth. Part of knowing your worth is only allowing individuals into your life that will help you grow.

Of course, we all have those going out friends who are great for going out. The ones that serve purely an entertainment purpose. And that's ok! During all stages of life, you will have those contacts that are come and go friends. I believe those people come into your bubble to teach you a lesson and help you grow even though they may not stick around long-term. But I encourage you to evaluate your day-to-day contacts, confidants and loved ones. Do they know how to push you past your limits, without leaving you feeling offended, angry, hurt, or attacked? Do they have your best interests at heart or are they self-serving? Is the relationship 50-50 or are you putting in all the work?

You will find the answers to these questions over time. We all experience personal growth through the relationships we form with others. As we get older, we begin to realize who we want to keep close and continue to grow with and who just met us along our way to impart us with a necessary piece of knowledge. As we continue on our personal development paths, it's important to remember that the good ones probably know us better than we know ourselves.

We do what we feel is necessary for survival, but they see our superhuman capabilities and our potential. If I lived every day in survival mode, which I often do, I would never leave my house because I'm afraid of everything. But people push and challenge me to be greater than I would normally allow myself to be. My parents push me. My friends push me. My colleagues push me. And more than anyone, my therapist pushes me. Yes, I adore and hate her for it at the same time.

I recommend identifying who these people are for you and holding onto them for dear life. If you can't find, then know I am here cheering you on and pushing you ahead. And best of all, know you have yourself. Be your own cheerleader. This book is all about honesty, so I'll tell you, I suck at this part personally, but sometimes you just gotta do it. Like I said earlier, make that list, know what you want to change, formulate a game plan, and pat yourself on the damn back as you crush your goals. I like to pat myself on the back with new yoga pants, which contributes to my budgeting issue, but that is neither here nor there. Celebrate, whoop for joy, and live it up. You will start to see how the changes you make begin to transform your life for the better and lead to a life full of contentment, satisfaction, and pride.

Carrie Thompson

PERFECTIONISM, GUILT, SHAME &
FORGIVENESS

Perfectionism. Guilt. Shame. Forgiveness. I wanted to write separately about all four of these, but I feel strongly that they're all interconnected. In different ways, they intertwine with one another and weave their way around all aspects of our life. I personally struggle with all four, with perfectionism being the umbrella for the other three.

I can't say precisely when it began, but for as long as I can remember, I've suffered with the need to be perfect. Then as time went on and I made choices that ended up in feelings of guilt and shame, my need to strive for my idea of perfection was elevated. I guess it's kind of like the chicken and the egg. Maybe the perfectionism isn't the umbrella, and it sits equally, upon its throne, looking down at me with the rest. I do know, however, that perfectionism and my constant need to be an overachiever affect every aspect of my life and contribute to my feelings of guilt and shame and my inability to forgive myself for anything.

From what I can gather, my idea of perfection began to form during childhood. The children I became friends with when I was young were all extremely intelligent. Many of them were entered into the gifted program in elementary school, but I did not. I can't remember if I ever actually took the test or whatever it was to get in, but it was something that always separated us. That small detail already planted the idea of being "less than" in my mind from a young age. I was also less popular, not as attractive nor as athletically inclined as some of my friends, most of which you already know.

I always strived to be on their level but couldn't quite get there. I found myself constantly chasing an image or skill set that I just could not achieve. It was frustrating and heart breaking. The development of this "I am lesser" thought pattern also led to many of my regretful behaviors, as it permeated my life beyond childhood. Looking back now, I realize I was very smart and talented in my own ways but was blind to that fact. I think many of us fall into this trap, and it becomes challenging to escape.

In addition, I was a private child and never expressed my feelings to my parents. If they would've known how much I was hurting inside and how lost and alone I felt, perhaps they would have stepped in. They've always been overwhelmingly supportive of my brother and my endeavors, praised our successes and held us up through our failures, but for a long time, I just did not feel comfortable opening up to them on that level. It would take years for me to gain that level of trust and begin to share how I felt inside.

I believe another contributor in my struggle with this perfectionism stuff, along with shame and guilt, has to do with my deeply religious, Catholic upbringing. If you grew up in a religious home, maybe some of this will resonate with you.

From the day I was born until the day I turned 18 and went to college, religion was a part of my life. My mom had a strict Catholic upbringing and was very traditional. My dad was also raised in Catholic home, but I don't think it was as rigid. I think a lot of good can come from being brought up this way. You're taught to respect others; love thy neighbor as thyself; give back to the community; respect yourself; don't be greedy; don't cheat, lie or steal; don't harm other people and respect your parents. Those are all excellent values and really should be followed by everyone.

But, depending on how you're raised and how you interpret things, you may believe that you shouldn't embrace your sexuality, women shouldn't get to choose what they do with their bodies, if you ever question your faith something is wrong with you, you shouldn't party, you shouldn't dress a certain way, you shouldn't live with a significant other before you get married, etc. These have been conflicting messages for me for my entire existence, even up to this moment in time, because I want to live the life of a good Christian but also remain authentic in who I am. I've also learned over time that religion doesn't always define the person. There are many Christians who are bad people and just as many atheists who are amazing humans. In my heart, I believe that if you try to be the best human you can be, and yes, that can mean living a life by God's word, and treat everyone with respect, including yourself, you are doing fine despite your personal views on life.

Now, if these are your beliefs and you're an extremely devout Christian (or any other religion for that matter) and you have a more flexible interpretation of the teachings than mine, more power to ya, sis! I think that is a beautiful thing and have wonderful friends that are extremely religious. The most important part is finding what works best for YOU. What in your life fills your heart and leads you on a path to being a decent human being? That's what matters. And I do fully believe there is a higher being out there, guiding us all on our path and giving us hope when there's not much else to hang on to.

I'm not here to argue for or against religion, because I do pray and am a Believer, but I have to talk about the impact that religion had on me, my thought processes and my expectations for myself. You also have to keep in mind that I see everything in black or white. I don't like the grey area. My therapist can tell you that. I've been like this for my entire life, so as I developed my belief system over time, there wasn't a lot of room for flexible interpretation. I take everything literally. It's another issue I work on in therapy, and it's a royal pain in the ass.

Because no one ever intervened, opened my mind to the grey and flexible area of thinking or tried to steer my developing ideas on perfectionism, these ideals I created became more ingrained in my mind. As the years passed, I longed more and more to be like my friends or celebrity role models I'd identified as ideal personalities. I grew more envious and jealous, my self-esteem worsened, my negative self-talk got out of control, I developed a nasty temper, and I was depressed. This led to college years full of scandalous and obnoxious behavior, all of which have been discussed in previous chapters.

After I graduated and reflected on all the mistakes I had made and embarrassing moments I couldn't stand to relive, I started trying to build this façade to hide behind. My first few years in Charlotte ended the same as my college days. Too much drinking. Too much partying. Distasteful behavior. And ramped up levels of envy and jealousy. A part of me was living life to the fullest, but a bigger part was absolutely disgusted in the person I'd become.

The disgust led to anxiety and the anxiety led to actions I'm not proud of. Sometimes it was unwarranted jealousy, sometimes it was anger, sometimes it was me shutting myself off from the world and backing out of prior obligations. Sometimes it was my being conniving or undercutting or just mean for no good reason other than I felt threatened by another person, typically a friend. My anxiety led me to constantly critique others and project my insecurities onto the world around me. It made me want to always be the best, even if that hindered other peoples' ability to advance. It made me want to hoard all the knowledge, skills, and attention, even though one of my favorite and most fulfilling activities is training other people.

This left me in a constant state of feeling conflicted. The person I wanted to be and the person I was were different in so many ways. I wanted to be somebody that people look up to or come to for advice or inspiration. I wanted people to think that I was kind, loving, inclusive, and happy. My goal was to spread happiness to other people, and I always wondered why or how I could do that if I couldn't even feel happy myself. Feeling conflicted about who you are and who you want to be can add to your anxiety and depression. Sometimes I had to ask myself "What can I do to become the person that I want to be, and why is it so difficult for me to become that person?"

Because of the disappointment I felt, I began trying to live a life that I thought would make me into my idea of a "good" person. I had this vision of what I should be, how I should act, what type of job I should have, the types of thoughts I should have, the way I should treat people, etc., and I was bound and determined to live and project that image. I wanted everyone to see me in this light and would do anything to keep it that way. I also wanted everyone to like me, and when someone didn't, it gave me immense amounts of anxiety.

Now don't get me wrong, I was never a "bad" person. I didn't go around treating people like shit or being a disrespectful asshole, but there were massive discrepancies between the life I thought I should be living and the life I was actually living. I thought I needed to be quiet, unseen, sweet to everyone, never have a nasty thought about anyone or anything, never complain, never say no, never gossip, never judge anyone, never be jealous, dress the "right" way, go to the right places, never party, have a successful career, excel at everything I try, never make a mistake, never hurt anyone's feelings, be good at every single activity I set out to do, always be a ray of sunshine and love everyone. If you think all that is insane, well, that's just the short list of expectations I had for being a "good" person or ideal person.

The expectations are not realistic. I kept reaching towards this idea of perfectionism that just wasn't achievable. If I'm being honest, this is still something I'm working through in therapy. I have convinced myself that people I know, and others out there are already living this "perfect" life being Mother Teresa. All good intentions, perfect personality, loved by all, spreading love and light to the world every moment, never having a negative thought or action and just being Sally Sunshine every day... I mean Lynn and Bria kind of are this way, but ha-ha .... you know... we all have flaws.

The reality is, from a young age I started building the idea of this perfect human based on what I had seen, been taught, read, and heard and just allowed it to get more complicated over time. Once we reached the age of social media, it got a lot worse. I think we can all agree that social media allows us all to portray the image we want the world to see, whether we show the whole picture or even a modicum of truth. And after putting all that out there, we proceed to consume unhealthy amounts, because all these apps are easily accessible. I'd be lying if I said I didn't go down a 30-minute Instagram hole at least once a week, or if we are honest, probably once a day.

If we aren't being prudent consumers, what we see gets engraved in our brains, and over time it starts affecting our reality. There's a damn good reason my therapist suggested a social media cleanse when I was insanely anxious every day. All that scrolling is not good for the self-esteem or the mind. The comparison games begin. You look at your friends or the other people you follow and think "Wow!

Look at their perfect life, job, relationship, marriage, body, house, car or children. I wish I had that." BOOM! You lose touch with what you already have in your life, forget to be grateful for the gifts life has already given you and feel like absolute crap because you don't have XYZ. It's nonsense, and we have to do better.

Anyway, all of this is to say:

1. I set unrealistic expectations for myself and the world around me.
2. Trying to hold myself to these standards made me a neurotic mess.
3. Something had to be done to chip away at these ideals I'd formed around perfectionism.

Once again, thank God for therapy. Once Ashley started to notice these perfectionistic tendencies, she started bringing them up over and over so we could start to chip away at these beliefs.

What I learned was nobody is perfect. My expectations were outrageous. I was allowed to make mistakes. In fact, many of the mistakes of my past weren't anything I should feel guilt or shame for, they were normal mistakes, normal choices made by your average teenager/college kid. All this time I had been beating myself up because I thought I was going to disappoint my family and friends if they knew the things I'd thought or done, but no. Most people I know were doing the same dumb crap that I was. Mind Blowing, right?! But not really.

Because I spent so much time beating myself up about my life choices, I lost sight of all of my admirable qualities. It was depressing to think about what a horrible person I was every day and led to me feeling unworthy of love or friendship. These beliefs also drove me crazy at work. I felt like if I ever made one little mistake, I was useless and would be fired. I hated feedback and worked myself into a tizzy every time I got review comments, because I thought I'd surely get in trouble if anything wasn't done to perfection. Wrong again.

Now I've learned to ask for feedback and appreciate the opportunities for growth provided through those conversations. I'm not as worried about making mistakes, so I make less mistakes and feel more confident when performing tasks. It's kind of wild how that works. It's important to remember that everyone is constantly learning. My boss is a genius and even she doesn't know it all. You gain so much from making those mistakes and asking the subsequent questions because you are setting yourself up to grow and excel at your career.

Now the tricky part. It's easy to say "Ok! We don't need to be perfect and we shouldn't feel guilt or shame about our life choices. But, like, I have to forgive myself to actually move on?" Yes, yes, we do, and it's not easy but it's a must. I struggle significantly with forgiveness and is a continual work in progress. And forgiveness is more than forgiveness of yourself. It's for yourself and others.

Learning to forgive yourself is more difficult than learning to forgive other people, in my opinion. With other people it is easy to just write them off or ignore them if you're struggling to forgive them. But you can't just do that with yourself, unfortunately. You are stuck with yourself 24 hours a day, seven days a week from the day you're born until the day you die. Because of this, you need to learn to forgive yourself and let go. It sounds simple enough, but not so much.

Most of the self-help books I've read emphasize the importance of letting go, and I'm sure that you've heard it as many times as I have from friends and family. "Just let it go." "Relax!" "Just forget about it." Every time I hear those words, I just wanna scream and pull my hair out. They aren't wrong, though. You do need to learn to let it go and most importantly to forgive yourself for things you've done in your past and even for things that you're doing in your present.

We have all gone through rough phases. We've had to make mistakes to learn lessons and those mistakes have helped us grow. But it's still not easy. It takes work. Everyday work. It takes a full on 24 hour a day commitment to yourself and to your progress. I struggled with this for a long time. Letting go was one of the most difficult things for me through my journey. I felt like I could just not forgive myself for all the dumb mistakes I made in the past. After realizing (aka being told my Ashley) that the actions I was most embarrassed and ashamed of were commonly made bad decisions for most young adults, I felt less alone.

Those realizations took off some of the pressure and gave me room to breathe. I realized I didn't have to hate myself so much. I was so wrapped up in what other people would think of me, that I ended up thinking horribly of myself when no one else probably gave a crap, and if they did, they shouldn't be in my life. I put so much energy into hiding the person of my past far from everyone's sight that I lost sight of who I am in the present. At some point I had to realize that if people weren't going to judge me based on the person I am now, I should not want them in my life.

I don't have any simple tips and tricks to make you magically forgive yourself and let go. What I can tell you is, know that you're not alone in your feelings. The things that you've done in your past have brought you to the person that you are in your today. Your experiences helped you to set goals and to realize things about yourself that you wanted to change. These experiences helped you to cross paths with people that have taught you lessons or maybe even became your closest friends. Growth is an ongoing process. No one is expected to get it right 100% of the time. That's reality, hunny. What matters is that you are continually to work on being the best person you can be and treating yourself, and others, with kindness every step of the way.

Carrie Thompson

FINDING YOUR PURPOSE

I have to start this section with a quote my yoga teacher, Camimi, said at one of her Monday night sunset classes during Savasana. This really resonated with me and is an affirmation we should all repeat to ourselves daily. "There is a place on this earth that only you can fill. Don't forget it." I think it's quite easy to get lost in the details of life going on around us, especially if you're constantly playing the comparison game, which I am guilty of myself. But it's true, sometimes it just takes a while to figure that out. There IS a place that ONLY you can fill. And you should never forget that.

You will notice in this section, I will use the words purpose and dream synonymously. It is my belief that fulfilling your life's purpose is the true dream come true, so I will speak to it that way.

I have found that one of the best ways to help yourself through anxiety and depression is by finding your purpose in life. We all have a purpose for being on this earth, but sometimes it is just not apparent. For years I struggled with figuring out my purpose in life. I felt like I was floundering every second, and I just didn't understand why I was here. It becomes much more difficult when you feel like you are struggling and suffering to get from day to day.

Anyone with an anxiety, depression or other mental health issue can probably relate to this. Of course, there are times when you feel good, when you are happy, and when all aspects of life seem to be going your way. However, for me the anxiety always drowned any of that out. The anxiety stuck out so much more than the good times and made me question myself. A lot of the times I would always come back to, "What is my purpose in this life?" I would always wonder why I am here and what I am doing if all I feel is anxious, sad, and lost. There are so many times when I felt alone and like all of my friends had their lives together.

Well one thing I learned was that no one fully has their life together. I also learned that you can never judge exactly what goes on in someone's life by looking at it from the outside. There's usually a lot more that goes on behind the scenes than you can ever know, and they may truly be on a journey similar to yours, feeling lost and alone. Social media makes it easy to get lost in this comparison spiral. If you aren't familiar with someone on a personal level, I challenge you to step back and remind yourself that all that glitters is not gold.

It took quite some time for me to even have a fleeting idea of what my purpose might be. Figuring it out wasn't as easy as just sitting down and thinking about it for a few minutes or a few hours. It wasn't even a few days or a few weeks. One day it just seemed to come to me. I feel like this might be how it is for a lot of people. I don't believe that purpose is a part of life that can be planned out. I believe that it is an innate part of your being. A collection of traits, experiences, interests, and ideas that are developed as we mature over time. Then one day, the light bulb goes off.

It happened for me during, what I consider to be, the craziest year of my life, and probably many other people's too. As you already know, my complete mental breakdown began in December of 2019 and continued well into the apocalyptic year of 2020. During a global pandemic, one frequently finds themselves pondering what their purpose is in life, especially when most of your days are spent working from home on your couch. I had struggled with this question for a long time, as I mentioned above, but in 2020 it hit me hard and added to my anxiety and the crazy toiling in my brain. But one ordinary Sunday in late spring it came to me. The day was picture perfect, so maybe this was a sign. Just to picture it now makes me smile. A beautiful, perfectly sunny day in the South. It was 80 degrees with no humidity, and I had a massage scheduled that I had completely forgotten about. During those magical 90 minutes with Jess, while she was digging her forearm down into my calf muscle, it came to me. Through the pain and suffering, only the kind that can be uniquely found in a deep tissue massage, I finally figured it out.

That ordinary, yet magical day, I realized that my purpose in life was to help others and to use my story and my experience to try to make other people feel a little bit better about themselves. To me, my purpose on this earth is to try to bring joy to every person I meet and to try to spread happiness at any opportunity that presents itself. I thought the best way to bring this purpose or vision to life was through a book. I've always had a passion for books and have been reading like a maniac since I was little. So, I thought to myself, why not write my own story! Finally figuring this out gave me a glimmer of hope and helped me through some of the darkest times.

Shit didn't get a whole lot easier. There were still a lot of rough days, but it made it easier to push forward now that I had my purpose to keep me going. I know that sometimes it's hard to believe that you have a purpose, especially when the shit hits the fan. But everyone has a purpose, even the worst among us live to serve as lessons of what not to do and what not to be.

For most of us though, our purpose is much greater than that. We don't just exist to take up space. It can be hard to see, especially when you're the one living through trauma or feeling just generally "stuck" in life. We just have to try and remember that other people may be depending on our gifts and may see us in a much brighter light then we can see for ourselves. If I could randomly figure mine out during a massage one day, I feel like this could happen for anyone. I encourage you to take that time to think about it a little bit. Sit down and journal. Maybe try a meditation or just some time with your eyes closed, where you go within and try to see what your soul is trying to tell you. If this isn't working for you, speak to your loved ones and people you trust.

After my little epiphany, I was still feeling somewhat uncertain. Living in a perpetual state of self-doubt is something I'd become quite accustomed to at that point. To give me confidence in this new knowledge, I reached out to my therapist and my friend Lynn. They're people I trust and know will be brutally honest. I told my therapist the thought that had come to me, and she was just as excited as I was, which I took to be a good omen. She thought that writing a book and sharing my story would be therapeutic for me and the people I could touch with the story. My conversation with Lynn was a little different. I asked her what she thought were some of my strongest qualities. And while I don't remember the message exactly, she alluded to the fact that I could always make people smile and feel happy or generally make people feel better about themselves. These reactions solidified the thoughts I'd had during and after my massage. Now it was time to make a game plan.

Like I said before it didn't take days or weeks or months for me even, but I never gave up and finally it came. Giving up seems like a better solution some days because it may feel easier. Even when you're miserable, sometimes it's more comfortable to stick with what you know because it's predictable. Leaving your comfort zone is scary and uncomfortable, but I encourage you to never give up on yourself. There's probably a dream out there that you didn't even realize you had just waiting to be discovered.

Once you've finally discovered your purpose, the real trick is learning to live your purpose. Researching how to make it happen and getting a game plan together so that you can execute will lead to success. You have to take it upon yourself to dig deep and figure out exactly what it's going to take to live that purpose and live the life that you want to have. The more that you are fulfilling your purpose every day, the more you will live a life full of meaning. It will give you that push when you feel like giving up. It will give you something to come back to when you feel like you have nothing to hold onto anymore.

It's good to discuss your purpose with the people who care about you and the ones that you trust the most. When the shit hits the fan, they'll always be the ones to remind you that your life is so much more than the challenges you are facing or the limitations you're placing on yourself. If you don't feel you have resources like this in your circle, try to find a club or group of like-minded individuals that share goals similar to yours. I know that I've personally found people that share my goals and interests just by listening to podcasts. Many of them have cult followings, and you never know, you might meet your next mentor or best friend if you get involved.

Surrounding yourself with the right people is an integral part of the process. Once I realized that I wanted to write a book, I started telling the people I knew would support me. I had a friend from Ohio State, Dr. Nicolya Williams, who is a bestselling author, and decided to reach out to her. Although I knew her and her beautiful little daughters were published authors, I had no idea how much of a resource she would become. Through a simple message to a long-lost friend, I stumbled upon a wealth of writing wisdom.

Dr. Nicolya had used her struggles and experience with writing her own books, along with her education, to run a book writing bootcamp course for aspiring authors. I knew right away that once my busy season at work calmed down, I would sign up and begin the process of writing this book. Had I never reached out, I would have been trying to figure this out all on my own. This just serves as an example that resources and help can be found in the most unlikely of places. Take the time to brainstorm people, groups or places you could gain knowledge from or assistance in chasing your dream.

Another valuable tool is to write it down. Write it all down. Write down your dream. Write it down with conviction. "I will be/am a bestselling author." "I will be/am a nurse." "I will be/am a nutritionist." Whatever your dream may be. Maybe your purpose in life is to grow your first garden in your backyard. "I am the best gardener in town." Not everyone's purpose has to be some earth shattering, do-gooder type of thing. What matters is that it feels important to YOU and that you feel confident in your ability to live your purpose and accomplish your dream. Affirm this for yourself every day. Then work through the steps of how you can get there. Write some more. List out what you want to do or think you should do to accomplish this dream. When you have the beginning blueprint, you will feel confident in your ability to begin this new chapter in life.

A plethora of resources exists on the interwebs. The internet is full of so much information that it's easy to get lost. Get recommendations from friends or acquaintances on where you can find information. If they aren't helpful, try my podcast idea again. There is a podcast for everything. Blogs and YouTube are other resources to check out. I guarantee that someone else has already set out to crush the same goal as yours, and one of those people probably talks about it online. If your idea is original, then you get to lead the way, and that is extremely admirable.

Once you've got your game plan, resources, and support system, it's time to do the damn thing. Don't procrastinate! I think a lot of us hold back because we are too concerned with other people's expectations of us, and that keeps us stagnant. But there's no need for that. No matter how scary it may be, just start to execute. Don't let fear, limiting beliefs and other people's expectations hinder you from going for the gold. If you don't at least try, you'll never know what you are capable of accomplishing. Waiting around never got anyone to the top. The most successful people out there work hard and never give up.

My next best advice is to never give up. Do you know how many times I wanted to give up on this book because I thought "No one will want to read your story." or "You're never going to get to 200+ pages." Too many times. However, I just kept on writing, because it felt good and I wanted to make myself proud.

Like with everything else in life, it's not going to be a cake walk. There will be ups and downs, tears, roadblocks, and sacrifice. You might lose some sleep, time with friends, night outs, Netflix time. You might disappoint some people and, hell, you may even fail. But regardless of the outcome, you will be so proud of yourself. Stay strong and push through until the very end, because eventually you will have that breakthrough and be successful in your endeavors. Then you can share your gifts with the world. The world needs your voice, your experience, your gifts. You are one of a kind, and no matter what you think of yourselves or how successful you feel, you may be inspiring someone else.

IT'S THE LITTLE THINGS

I wanted to include a chapter to give you all the little tips and tricks I've discovered over the years, the small but comforting activities I've learned to engage in and some short stories that have resulted in enormous amounts of happiness, inner peace, accomplishment, and gratitude. I share in hopes that you take the time to reflect on these types of activities or memories in your life and find immense amounts of joy in those ponderings.

1.   Family is everything. You may hold some grudges against your parents or siblings for things in the past, but when shit hits the fan, they can be your best resource. I could not have survived this last year without my parents and brother and cherish every minute I spend with them. I'll never forget when, in the midst of my breakdown and beginning to try medication, I received a package from Amazon in the mail. I didn't remember ordering anything, but when I opened it, it was a book and a journal my brother had sent me with a sweet note just to bring a little sunshine to my day. I immediately started sobbing, and my mom asked me what was wrong. I was just so overwhelmed with gratitude and love for his support that it brought me to tears. I'm blessed beyond belief and wouldn't trade them for the world. And family doesn't have to mean blood relatives. Sometimes it's just the people you love the most, who you can depend on and who will always be there to support you on your journey.

2.   Find your tribe and always keep them close. It is not always easy to find quality friends, so when you do, make sure you hold em' tight and let them know how much they mean to you. I cannot tell you how grateful I am to get to live this life with my people. My girls Lynn, Connie, Adasha, Clarisse, Amber, Bria, Chelsea 1, Chelsea 2, Chelsea

3, Kelsey, Megan, Jen, Tina, Abby, Gina, Kathryn, Jen, Nikki, Jen Jen and Kier (amongst many others) kept me sane during all of this. They checked up on me all the time and would never let me wallow for too long. They encouraged me to keep pushing forward and reassured me that one day, I would finally feel like myself again. My friend Mikey let me cry to him on more than one occasion, reassuring me that I was most certainly not a burden to my friends and family and that he would be by my side no matter what, loving me while I was broken just as much as any other time. No matter how down in the dumps I felt, these people never stopped inviting me to events, never stopped reaching out and stuck by my side as I reentered the world after my breakdown. Keep your people close. Tell them how much you love them all the time and stick together no matter what.

3. Be open minded when it comes to meeting new people. If you have been burned in the past by friends, which I think we all probably have before, it can be hard to trust new people. This is even more difficult if you're an introvert and would rather hole up at home with your pet and a glass of wine, but hear me out. A few years ago, one of my best friends from college, Kathryn, asked me to be in her wedding and then, of course, her bachelorette party. This party would include her and four other girls I'd never met, in fact most of us had never met one another. We were all friends from different stages of her life, including childhood, college, and present times. You may be thinking, "Oh hell. Mixing a bunch of women that have never met and including alcohol is never a good idea." Wrong! After a weekend in New Orleans, a mutual dislike of a crazy girl who doesn't believe that dinosaurs ever existed, and lots of alcohol and stories, I ended up with the three best friends a girl could ever have. The four of us talk almost daily in our "Dino Girls" group chat and have kept our love of dinosaurs and inside jokes going for over two years now. I encourage you to keep your heart open, because not everyone is out to get you and you never know when you might stumble upon one of your soulmates.

4. Self-care is an absolute freaking must. I know balling on a budget can be hard, but it is crucial to treat yourself every now and then when it comes to self-care. Draw yourself a bath, light some candles, throw in some essential oils or a bath bomb and grab a glass

186

of wine or cup of tea and shut out the world for 20 minutes. Treat yourself to a manicure or pedicure or buy some nice nail polish and have a little DIY night. I always feel better when my nails are done. Treat yourself to a high-quality face mask. Buy yourself a weighted blanket. I cannot stress enough how much comfort my blanket has brought me. It's like snuggling up in one giant, comforting hug. The best part is, it is a one-time upfront cost and lasts forever. Keep your eye on the GMA Deals website, as they often have them on sale.

Get your hair done. Get a massage. Go to a wellness center for a restorative stretch or cryotherapy. I always keep my amazing wellness team on speed dial. Jess always gets my hair looking like perfection, Laura, my goddess chiropractor fixes all my aches from sitting at a computer all day and my other Jess is a unicorn massage wizard. I make sure I set aside time and money where I can get in my appointments, turn off my phone for a bit and just relax and unplug.

5.   Exercise is a lifesaver. I am a fitness fanatic, but you don't need to be a fanatic to move your body. There are so many benefits to spending 30 minutes a day getting some movement in. You can get in an ass kicking HIIT workout at your favorite boutique fitness studio. If you're in Charlotte, I highly recommend West Kept Secret. Another convenient option is grabbing a challenging workout off YouTube to break a sweat in your living room. Sydney Cummings has been a lifesaver for me when I want to workout at home or bring my workouts on the road.

BUT it doesn't have to be all that. Go support your local yoga teacher at an outdoor class. Grab a friend and go for a walk or a hike. And if life is just too much already and you can't bring yourself to get moving, try stretching for 10 minutes. Find some beginner yoga poses online, do some breath work, and get in those restorative slow movements. All of these will get those endorphins boosting and improve your mood. Fitness is so much more than just physical health and appearance. It's guaranteed to help your mental, too.

6.   Beware of alcohol. When I first started having anxiety issues, I swore I'd never stop drinking. It seemed like some impossible sacrifice that would ruin my social life. After years of binge drinking,

wasting money, making stupid choices, and waking up feeling like death, I finally realized that a reduced intake of alcohol didn't mean sacrificing my social life. I had to give up alcohol for months when I first started having anxiety and then again during my mental breakdown. After months of not drinking, still spending time with friends, and having just as much fun as before, I realized that life without alcohol meant the same amount of enjoyment and less anxiety. Using alcohol to relax usually creates more anxiety the next day, hangover anxiety if you will. You'll sleep better without it, wake up ready to take on the world and spend way less money. Treat yourself to some nice self-care with those dollars you save.

7.   Find your escape. People always told me to journal, meditate, listen to anxiety podcasts, read anxiety books, yada yada yada. I tried to do all those things at once and none of them worked. Once I stopped trying everything everyone else recommended, I finally found what worked for me. I did start listening to podcasts, but ones about true crime and empowered women.

My first love is My Favorite Murder. Back in 2019, when I was trying to overcome the anxiety related to my heart scare and get settled back into therapy, I found My Favorite Murder. I had heard friends and coworkers gush over this podcast for months, but was never really a podcast girl, so I didn't listen. I finally got on the bandwagon, and from then on, I couldn't stop listening. It became an addiction. I would listen to more than one episode in a day. I have loved true crime from a young age, so this was right up my alley. As I cruised through the episodes, my love and obsession grew. They talked openly about their struggles with mental health and preached the importance of being true to yourself and loving you as you are. These women are badass feminists that stand for equality. They support the LGBTQ+ community and Black Lives Matter. They stand up for women's rights and fight against racism, sexism, etc. They keep it real, are hilarious and provide me weekly true crime indulgences.

Obviously, they are my absolute jam, but I also am in LOVE with Morbid, Sofia with an F, Call Her Daddy, Last Podcast on the Left and This is Why We Drink.

8.   Learn to meditate. I have to admit, I struggled with this one for years because…perfectionism. I finally realized that meditation isn't about being perfect. It's called meditation "practice" for a reason. You're continually learning and growing, so don't give up. If you look closer at the cover, the girl is scrunching her forehead because meditation is a struggle sometimes. That's supposed to depict me in one of those frustrating moments that have happened so many times. I promise that if you start a practice and stick with it, it will pay off over time. I recommend starting with the Calm app. There is a 30-day introduction to meditation that my friend Amber recommended to me. It's great and will help guide you and keep you from being discouraged.

9.   Read. Books are my great escape. Since I was a little girl, I constantly had a book in my hand, and nothing has changed since then. There are so many genres available today and new books coming out all the time that I guarantee you find something to your liking. Books take you to another place. They get you out of your head and transport you to another realm. They are one of my favorite ways to stave off an anxiety attack or to unplug before bed. My greatest suggestion is to have a technology free hour before bed where you are just reading and decompressing. It will help you sleep much more deeply and fall asleep more quickly. If you follow me, I will start putting book recommendations up and am always open for questions or recommendations!

10.   Find a type of journaling that works for you. It used to bug the hell out of me when people would tell me to "just journal and meditate." Yeah, no. That didn't work for me. Eventually I found a method that worked for me and brought a little joy into each day. Every night before bed, I write down at least four or five things from that day that I'm grateful for and then write five to ten affirmations. It's really cool to look back and see what amazing things have occurred over time in your life and reflect back on whether some of your affirmations came true. Note: The gratitude items don't have to be earth shattering every time. Yes, sometimes you'll be able to write something amazing like "I got engaged" or "I passed XYZ certification", but other times, it may simply be "I made it through today." Keep it genuine and simple.

11. Find comfort in the familiar and keep returning every time you feel overwhelmed or down in the dumps. Back in 2015, when I was first trying to navigate the waters of my newly diagnosed Generalized Anxiety Disorder, I leaned heavily on Harry Potter. There was just something about Harry Potter that brought me comfort and a sense of calm. I'm not sure why that was, maybe it's the childhood nostalgia that brought me back to simpler times, but whatever it was it did the trick.

Whenever I was feeling anxious, I would bury myself in the books and reread them, reliving the memories of Harry, Ron, and Hermione that I had read so many years ago. On the weekend nights when I didn't feel comfortable surrounded by friends, I would put on one of the many movies and live their lives through the big screen. I think my parents are completely burnt out at this point for the amount of times I've made them watch the movies. Whenever they would come on Freeform, I would record them on my parent's DVR so I could watch them endless amounts of times. I always hear a heavy sigh these days when I ask if we can watch Harry Potter during one of my weekend sleepovers, because they've seen the movies hundreds of times now thanks to me and my anxiety, but they give in when I ask.

Every time I reach a particularly tough patch in life, I come back here. I revisit the magical land J.K. Rowling developed for us and let my mind dive into the wonders that Harry Potter has to give. The books never get old and the stories welcome me back like an old friend. I recommend identifying your comfort activity and repeating whenever necessary.

12. Wellness dates are the best way to spend time with your friends. My friend Amber and I started having what we called "wellness dates" because we wanted to spend time together that didn't involve getting drunk. Before my breakdown, girls' nights involved a lot of alcohol, passing out on the couch at like 2am and waking up feeling like death the next day. After I started anxiety medication and stopped drinking for a while, I realized I wanted more quality forms of entertainment. Don't get me wrong, I love a good Sunday Funday or girls wine night, but there's something special about a wellness date

with your best pal.

Amber and I have done yoga dates, gone to body restoration spas, workout classes, coffee dates and yes, we have had wine nights too. After a while, I started roping in all my other friends. At first, I was afraid they wouldn't be into it, but these dates turned out to be a fan fav amongst my girls, and the memories we make are just as great as our nights out at the club used to be.

13. Put time into chasing your dreams or starting a new hobby that you've always thought about. This one doesn't take much explanation. During everyone's 2020 Coronacation, so many people began pursuing hobbies they'd never tried before. My friends were doing needlepoint, painting, writing poetry, learning some DIY home improvement, or starting small businesses. This book was the dream I didn't even know I had, and when the idea presented itself, I just knew I had to chase it hard. Find your something and go get it.

14. One of the lessons I'm still learning, and think is so important is this: Other people do not get to dictate how they made you feel. Only you and you alone can decide how you were feeling at any point in time. They may not agree with how their behavior impacted you or how you received a message from them, but your feelings are your feelings, end of story. I had a lot of concerns while writing this book about potentially hurting certain people's feelings or causing them to be angry at me or talk shit about me/my book. But you know what, I can't worry about that.

I was not about to let the opinions of a handful of people hinder my ability to succeed and tell my story, because it's exactly that, MY story, not theirs. Was my aim to be vindictive or hurtful? Hell no! Could I possibly piss someone off or hurt their feelings? Absolutely! But this is my story about my journey, and if I wanted to be 100% genuine and honest, I had to tell it from my point of view.

15. This is one of my favorites, and I have to give credit to Tana Mongeau on her words from the 103rd episode of Call Her Daddy. Comparison is the root of all evil, plain and simple. Stop comparing your life to everyone around you, because you can never really know

what's going on behind closed doors or in someone's head. Keep your eye on the prize. That prize is your own life. If you spend all your time admiring the lives of others, you will look back and wonder where the hell time went and what you could've accomplished to make yourself proud. Eyes forward, chin high, gratitude overflowing.

16. Learn to be content with the mundane. In a random discussion with Ashley, I realized what a key part this contentment plays in becoming genuinely happy. The big milestones and "Aha" moments are few and far between. For most of us, 80% or more of our lives are spent sloshing through the day to day. A large part of traveling through everyday life, is finding joy in every moment you can.

For me, it's the little things. It's waking up with my fluffy baby snuggled up with me, trips to the grocery store with my dad, a kick ass workout with my girl Sydney Cummings on YouTube or a Peloton ride with my PeloPeeps, baking cookies that turn out perfectly, long summer evening walks with my momma or buying someone the perfect gift and seeing the smile on their face. It's my weekly FaceTime calls with Jen just because, a surprise phone call from Clarisse, receiving a card in the mail from a loved one, logging on after a PTO day with less than five missed emails (actually rare and very exciting) or simply having that extra hour at bedtime to read my book.

I challenge you to find one thing each day that brings you joy, even if it's as simple as making the perfect pancake for breakfast or not stepping on a Lego your kid left on the floor. Over time, I promise this will create a magnificent impact to how you feel and bring lots more smiles to your face.

17. Courage is not the absence of fear and discomfort. Courage is having the fear and discomfort and continuing to push forward, all the way through to the other side. This can be a tough one for some of us, me included.

Do any of you have a seemingly automatic response/reaction when attempting anything new in various areas of your life? Any time I'm afraid of the outcome, I hesitate to move forward with my dreams and desires. I'm also known to give up right away if something doesn't work out for me on the first try, I believe accomplishing the goal will be challenging or I may not be able to accomplish the goal right away. And for the record, I'm always scared or dreaming up worst case scenarios. Sometimes I never move forward, and sometimes I wait until I have encouragement from multiple people before I take the leap. Do NOT do this.

Don't be afraid to try something new, and more importantly, don't be afraid of failure. As cliché as it may sound, you'll never know what you can accomplish until you try. Don't sell yourself short by not taking your first step just because you're scared.

18. Accepting the possibility that something could happen does not mean you want it to happen, nor does it mean it will or will not happen. Some of what occurs in our lives is not under our control. We can only control how we react to what happens. This includes accepting all possibilities and dealing with life's events as they occur instead of spending hours worrying and wishing the worst away.

19. Don't stay in situations that make you unhappy just because you're comfortable. This may be a job, friendship, or relationship. Perhaps you're afraid of what will happen if you step away from something so familiar out into the unknown. That's ok. We all feel that way sometimes. The issue is, you don't want to look back and wonder what could've been had you taken the steps to make a change for the better. It's ok to walk away. It's ok if your decision to move upsets other people. You are not responsible for their lives and their feelings. You're responsible for you. Honor yourself by letting go of what does not serve you and starting a life that brings you peace and joy.

20. Time in nature is healing. It's a proven fact. Put down the cell phone and step outside. Breathe in the fresh air. Admire the beautiful trees, flowers, and wildlife. Go to the beach or the mountains and take in all the wonders of the earth. Dig your toes in the sand or stand in the grass, focusing on the sensation on your feet. Listening to the waves or the birds chirping in the trees. Smell the salty air or the damp leaves and earth beneath your feet. Close your eyes, breathe deep and thank mother nature for all we have been given. Take her in with all

of your senses and let go of whatever hangs heavy on your soul. It is grounding, cleansing and will bring you peace.

21. Be spontaneous every now and again. If you're anxious like me and prefer to stick to a routine, I really want you to push yourself to do this more frequently. Take a random road trip, fly to see a friend, take a day off and just do whatever your heart desires. Throw the calendar and the daily to-do list out the window. The work will be there when you get back. Your house can wait another week to be cleaned. That massage appointment ... yeah, you can move that, too. You never know what memories await. Plus, sticking to a schedule and routine all the time is boring, and we could all use a little shake up sometimes. Making spontaneity a habit might help improve your anxiety, as well. You will learn how much fun you can have when you let your guard down and let loose.

22. Panic Attack Survival 101: If you wake up in the middle of the night with a panic attack, I recommend a cold shower, cold water on your face, a quick walk around your house, drinking cold water, taking deep breaths for 2-3 minutes or turning on a calming meditation and really listening to the words while you work on slowing your breath. I encourage you to gently remind yourself that it will pass. I often like to repeat over and over "I am not in danger, just discomfort" as a reminder that I'm physically ok and will feel relief soon.

This used to happen to me all the time and terrified the crap out of me. Sometimes it'd be bad enough that I'd drive to my parents' house at 2 and 3 in the morning, freaking out about what was going on. By the time I got there, my heart rate had slowed, and the adrenaline rush calmed down. I'd be perfectly fine and got all worked up for nothing. Try to stay calm, utilize the tips above and just lean into it. The less you fight it off, the quicker it will go away.

23. Dizziness, nausea, shortness of breath, a tight chest, pounding heart and twitching eyes are normal, especially when you're having a particularly high stress, high anxiety period of life. Sometimes these symptoms are a sign of an oncoming panic attack. If the physical sensations start escalating, try the tips listed above. Accepting what is coming is the easiest way to move through the attack. I also find it's

helpful to redirect my attention to something like a podcast, music, reading, or work. It helps to redirect my brain away from the doomsday thinking and puts me back on track.

24. If you're anxious or depressed, don't be nervous to communicate what you're experiencing to other people, especially those you love and trust. No one is a mind reader, although this is a superpower, I wish I possessed. I recognize it can be challenging to openly talk about mental health issues. However, we cannot expect others to understand why we feel how we feel, act how we act or make the choices we make if we don't inform them. Maybe you feel embarrassed or afraid they will think less of you because you have these struggles. Often, they will be able to relate. If they're not empathetic, then screw them. See #19. Leave those fools that aren't serving you. You don't need people like that in your life! We need to combat the stigmas around mental health and normalize honest conversations about mental health. Speaking up increases awareness, which will not only help you but others suffering as well.

25. Love the ever-living shit out of yourself. Love yourself during every single phase of your life. I don't care if you just made the most horrific mistake or achieved your highest life goal. You deserve love and kindness every day, NO MATTER WHAT!

THE END

If there's one thing I learned during the process of writing this book is if I can survive a mental breakdown, medication experimentation, mom's cancer, the 2020 COVID pandemic, the 2020 election and well … just 2020 in general, anyone can survive anything. You just have to know that you're worth the fight. Life is hard and full of all kinds of surprises and challenges, some of which we could never dream up on our own. But we were put here, equipped to survive and to do even more than that. We were put here to THRIVE. Having a mental illness can magnify everyday challenges 100 times their normal size, but you know what, that makes us better fighters.

I cannot tell you the amount of times that I wanted to give up because it all just became too overwhelming. I didn't think I could get past all the thoughts that weighed on me so heavily. I cried numerous times in therapy, to my family, to my friends and alone on my couch because I just didn't know what to do. And this is all perfectly normal. Everyone, and I mean everyone, has a breaking point. We just all reach it differently. But YOU are strong enough to traverse through the dark, scary woods and make it to the other side. You get to dream up your own paradise here. The light is waiting for you, I promise. And know in your mind, body, and soul that you CAN do it, you ARE worth it, and you WILL feel like a badass for continuing to move forward even when you don't think it's possible.

I appreciate you for taking the time to read my story, and I truly hope it made you feel like you have a kindred spirit out there in the world. Be proud of who you are. Speak up about mental health on behalf of yourself and of others out there fighting the good fight. We are in this together and will be until the very end.

ABOUT THE AUTHOR

Carrie is a Certified Public Accountant with a Bachelor's in Strategic Communications from The Ohio State University and a Master of Accounting from Winthrop University.

During her undergrad, she took great interest in Sociology and Women's Studies, peppering many of these classes throughout her course work. Learning more about the innerworkings of the human mind and human interactions contributed to her developing passion for people.

While Carrie loves her career, she is most fulfilled by her ability to connect with others. After being diagnosed with generalized anxiety disorder and diving into the world of mental health, she wanted to get more involved with mental health awareness. Through sharing her story, she hopes to encourage others to open themselves up and brave the discussions around mental illness.

Writing this book is Carrie's first step towards a professional life in the mental health realm. With goals of completing a life coach certification this year, she hopes to help others transform their lives for the better and find true contentment and joy.

In her spare time, Carrie enjoys riding her Peloton, spending time with friends and family, reading, baking, and playing with her kitty, Albie.

For more information, you can follow her on Instagram at @carriethompsonauthor and on Facebook at Carrie Thompson Author.

Made in the USA
Las Vegas, NV
20 February 2021